GET STARTED IN WRITING SCIENCE FICTION AND FANTASY

Adam Roberts

Get Started in Writing Science Fiction and Fantasy

Adam Roberts

First published in Great Britain in 2014 by John Murray Learning. An
Hachette UK company.

First published in US in 2014 by The McGraw-Hill Companies, Inc.

This edition published in 2014 by John Murray Learning

Copyright © Adam Roberts 2014

The right of Adam Roberts to be identified as the Author of the Work
has been asserted by him in accordance with the Copyright, Designs
and Patents Act 1988.

Database right Hodder & Stoughton (makers)

The *Teach Yourself* name is a registered trademark of Hachette UK.

British Library Cataloguing in Publication Data: a catalogue record for
this title is available from the British Library.

Library of Congress Catalog Card Number: on file.

Paperback ISBN 978 1 444 79565 3

eBook ISBN 978 1 444 79566 0

10 9 8 7 6 5 4 3

The publisher has used its best endeavours to ensure that any
website addresses referred to in this book are correct and active at
the time of going to press. However, the publisher and the author
have no responsibility for the websites and can make no guarantee
that a site will remain live or that the content will remain relevant,
decent or appropriate.

The publisher has made every effort to mark as such all words which
it believes to be trademarks. The publisher should also like to make
it clear that the presence of a word in the book, whether marked or
unmarked, in no way affects its legal status as a trademark.

Every reasonable effort has been made by the publisher to trace the
copyright holders of material in this book. Any errors or omissions
should be notified in writing to the publisher, who will endeavour to
rectify the situation for any reprints and future editions.

Typeset by Cenveo® Publisher Services.

Printed and bound in Great Britain by CPI Group (UK) Ltd., Croydon,
CR0 4YY.

John Murray Learning policy is to use papers that are natural,
renewable and recyclable products and made from wood grown in
sustainable forests. The logging and manufacturing processes are
expected to conform to the environmental regulations of the country
of origin.

John Murray Learning

338 Euston Road

London NW1 3BH

www.hodder.co.uk

Also available
in ebook

This book is dedicated to the staff of the Costa Coffee located at Martin's Heron, near Bracknell in Berkshire, where it – just like many other things its author has published – was written. With gratitude.

Contents

About the author

Adam Roberts has published 15 science-fiction novels, and a whole bunch of other stuff including short stories, novellas, parodies, criticism and reviews. Among his most recent books are: Jack Glass (2013), winner of the BSFA Award for Best Novel and the John W. Campbell Award; with Mahendra Singh, Twenty Trillion Leagues under the Sea (2014); and Bête (2014). He lives a little way west of London with his wife and two children, and has no cats. Since the majority of authors require a day job to cover all the bills, he has one of those: he is Professor of Nineteenth-century Literature at Royal Holloway, University of London.

How to use this book

I'll begin by making some assumptions about you – yes, you, holding this book in your hand. I'm assuming that you are interested in writing science fiction. And I'm assuming something more: that what you are looking for in this book is good, practical advice, such that by the time you have finished reading it you are not only writing science fiction but writing good, original, absorbing and thought-provoking science fiction. To that end you don't want me to peddle you cliché, vague generalities, impossible demands on your time or imagination. I'm not here to tell you what you *can't* do.

What this book is here to do is start you writing a memorable SF short story or novel. Each chapter will take you through a different part of this process, setting out in easily digestible chunks what you need to do, why you need to do it and, most importantly of all, how you need to do these things. There will be bullet points and exercises, anecdotes from my own experiences as a writer, hints, tips, pointers and suggestions. Chapters include sidebars that explain key terms and concepts used in science fiction and fantasy writing.

In what follows, I sprinkle 'story ideas' throughout as liberally as I can. I do this to illustrate one of my main beliefs about being a writer – namely that ideas are easy, and the 'having cool science fiction/fantasy ideas' ought not to hold you up. Now, since there is no copyright on 'ideas', that means you are free to use, explore, remix or otherwise exploit any story ideas you find in this book. I actively encourage you to do precisely that. If any of these story ideas grab you, then please run with them. But better yet would be to start having your own ideas.

In keeping with the 'Get Started in...' ethos, the emphasis throughout will be practical – on actually writing, rather than on general observations or abstractions.

Although I do discuss rules at several points in what follows, the purpose of this book is not to lay down rules you must follow. My actual purpose can be summed up in one phrase: to get you writing. Once you are writing, and especially once you are in the habit of writing, everything else becomes easier. Rules can help, if only to provide you with structure; but you will measure your success as a writer of science fiction and fantasy by the extent to which you can soar past the limitations the very word 'rules' implies.

So: if you write on a computer, open a new file on your machine in which to store all the things you are going to write. If you write with a pen on paper – you old traditionalist, you! – then buy a new notebook to dedicate to these exercises.

The exercises themselves are designed to be done in reasonably short slots of time. Another assumption I am making (there I go again!) is that you are relatively time poor – that you will have, as most writers have, many other calls upon your time: job, family, social life and so on. You are entitled to all three of those things, and shouldn't have to give them up to be a writer. But you will have to get used to syphoning off as much time as possible to the writing game. If you do all the exercises, you will end up with a folder (or notebook) containing half a dozen original short stories, a plethora of ideas and sketches for longer projects, various exploratory sentences, descriptions and dialogue snatches that might come in useful for later writing: a resource, in other words. Of course, if it so happens that you're in the fortunate position of being time rich rather than time poor, then hurrah! You can devote as much time as you like to being a writer. Speaking as somebody who is constantly struggling to find time to write around the demands made by having a day job, a family *and* a social life, I envy you!

I'm kidding! Kidding! I have no social life.

As this book is going to introduce you to the business of writing science fiction, it must also introduce you to the business of writing as a whole. I do not believe that science fiction is something you add on to writing as a kind of afterthought, like chocolate sprinkles on to your Starbucks Mocha. Writing science fiction means baking-in the 'SF-ness' from the beginning. It means using the toolkit of science fiction to express things which more mundane writing is incapable of getting at. But writing science fiction *is* writing; and so before we get to more genre-specific things I'm going to say something about that. To be more specific, I'm going to say three things, and I'd be grateful if you could commit them to memory. They're not long or complicated things, but they are crucial.

To find out what they are, you need to plunge into Chapter 1.

KEY TO SYMBOLS AND FEATURES

 Snapshot – a brief (usually five-minute) exercise

 Write – an exercise to take your writing forward

 Edit – the opportunity to rework and improve something you have done

 Workshop – longer, structured writing exercise

 Key quote – what others have had to say

 Key idea – the most important element to grasp

 Focus point – advice to take forward and apply to what you write

Where to next? – outlines what we're going to cover in the next chapter

SF Plotto – *Get Started in Writing Science Fiction and Fantasy* includes a random plot-point accumulator and story-generator called 'Plotto'. You'll find this at the end of the book, and you are invited to use it in order to generate your plots.

1

How to write

Let's not beat around the bush. I'll start by laying out the whole truth and secret of successful writing in words of (with two exceptions) one syllable. There's a bronze, a silver and a gold rule to writing, and here they are:

- Bronze rule: You must write, and finish what you write.
- Silver rule: You must revise what you write.
- Gold rule: Show, don't tell.

If you bear with me, I'll explain in more detail why these seemingly bland bromides are so very, very important.

You may be nodding sagely at these three 'rules'; or you may be tutting with annoyance that such how-to book clichés should be foisted on you so early on – you may believe that the very idea of rules is a ridiculous straightjacket and that all rules should be repudiated. If so, bravo! More power to you. I think you're wrong, and below I explain why I think that. But you don't have to listen to me – provided, only, that you have found a workable way of getting from 'ideas in your head' to 'finished written product that people love'.

You must write, and finish what you write

The bronze rule is perhaps so obvious as to not even need stating, except that there are many people in this world who prefer the *idea* of being a writer to the practical business of actual writing. Not you: you know better. But you know the type I'm talking about: the people who daydream about reclining on their yacht, casting an idle eye over their latest masterpiece which is topping the bestseller list. Or, to be less hyperbolic, they are the people who fancy meeting others at dinner parties and saying 'Me, oh, I'm a writer' and basking in their admiration. You are not so foolish as to indulge such nonsense. You know that writing is not a very efficient route to multi-millions; and that if it is money you are after, there are many better ways of getting it.

Nonetheless, there is a version of this evasion particularly common to science fiction – the individual who is happiest planning what she is going to write, rather than actually writing it. In science fiction this can take the form not only of drawing up detailed chapter breakdowns, but of drawing maps and star charts, inventing alien languages and sketching cool futuristic laser rifles and spaceships. All these things may well have a place in your story, but doodling around your story, even with the best intentions, is not a substitute for writing your story.

One of the crucial things that makes science fiction different from other kinds of writing is that it can play with big ideas and include cool imaginary kit.

But books are not made out of ideas.

Books are not made out of imagined worlds, or cool spaceships, or robots, or time machines.

Books are not made out of characters, however carefully you establish their family tree and sketch out their physical appearance.

Books are not made out of feelings, or convictions, or events.

Books are made out of words.

I'll repeat that. Books are made out of words.

We can be more specific: books are made out of the words the reader reads.

A writer is somebody who writes. The uncomfortable aspect of this truth is that, if you aren't writing (when you are playing goofing off, but even when you are planning and sketching and daydreaming about writing), you aren't a writer. But there's an upside too: as soon as you start putting words next to one another you are a writer, right up there with Tolstoy, J.K. Rowling and your favourite SF author. And while quite a lot of this book will be about encouraging you to treat 'rules' with a healthy suspicion, here is one rule that is engraved upon tablets of ultra stone and must not be broken. Write! Write as often as you can. Get into a routine that works for you – find a time of day (morning, afternoon, night-time after the kids have been put to bed, 45 minutes during your lunch break, whenever), arrange whatever aids you need (a cup of coffee, an extra strong mint, a pan-galactic gargle-blaster), pick up your pen, open your laptop and put the words down. Do whatever you need to do to make this happen: some writers like to tweet or Facebook their #amwriting daily totals; some are more private. It doesn't matter *how* you write; it doesn't even matter (in the first instance) *what* you write. It only matters *that* you write.

Write but a page a day, and by the end of the year you will have produced a 365-page novel. In fact, if you'd started a year ago, you'd already have written your novel! Think back in time to a year ago today: what was happening that meant you couldn't draft a page a day from that time until now? Nothing, right? So there's no reason to put it off any longer.

H.G. Wells

'I had rather be called a journalist than an artist.'

'What about writer's block?' I hear you ask. And my answer is: 'There is no such thing as writer's block.' That statement might seem to fly in the face of common sense. It might even look callous to people who are struggling to get the words down. But it's true, nonetheless. Think about it: do you think carpenters get 'carpenter's block'? Do hairdressers get 'hairdresser's block'? Do taxi drivers get taxi-driver block? ('Take me to 227 Playfair Street', 'I'd love to, sir, I really would; but I'm just feeling really *blocked* about my driving at the moment …') Writing *is* an art, but it is an art built upon craft; and craftspeople don't get craftsperson's block.

'But writing is different!' you say, and you add an exclamation mark for emphasis.

And, of course, it is.

The key to banishing 'writer's block' is to understand what it is. It is not the fear of the blank page, the awful chasm of existential disempowerment, the 'I can't think what to say until the muse moves me.' The word for that sort of thinking is 'self-indulgence'. (This may look like two words, but I consider the hyphen to meld the two components into one.) If that has been your problem, then you're in luck! The book you hold in your hand is filled with exercises, workshop tasks and specific ideas of what to write. By concentrating on those, instead of on yourself, you will work through whatever is holding you up.

But self-indulgence isn't the same thing as writer's block. The block is something else. It is that little voice in your head that chimes in as you finish a sentence, the voice that states 'Well, *that's* not a very good sentence; the voice that says: 'They're all going to *laugh* at you for writing such garbage'; that says: 'Better give up before you make things worse.' As a result, you stare into space feeling like a fraud and a failure; or else you spend three hours wrestling with the sentence in an increasingly desperate attempt to lick it into shape.

Focus point

One of the main strategies of SF is the literalization of metaphor. Take something that is in normal usage only a figure of speech and imagine how it would work as an actual thing: how would our current world have to change to accommodate it? How would people handle it? 'Writer's block' is one such. What would a literal writer's block look like?

Imagine, say, a future where writers are linked via brain implants to a central information processing system; and where any unspeakable ideas are blocked with a literal neuronal block at the point of origin. How might a writer get past that? Let's say she manages to, and her expression of the unspeakable triggers the blocks in all the other writers, leaving her the only writer supplying the complaisant global audience of story-suckers? How might she use that power – for personal gain, or something more idealistic? How would the system kick back?

That's not the way. The way is to silence that voice.

Everybody has that voice. All writers have to deal with it, no matter how fluent or successful they seem to the outside world. Indeed, in its place it's a good and necessary thing, The Voice, provided only that it comes at the right time in the process. When you are revising your work, you need to listen to your inner critic. But when you are writing your work, you must on no account let The Voice undermine you.

To speak for myself, I silence The Voice by listening to music while I write; I'm not sure how, but it holds the inner critic at bay long enough for me to get my first draft down. Other writers find other ways of ignoring it, with whatever version of 'Yes, yes, I'll get to your objections later' is effective for them.

You can take strength and comfort from this crucial piece of wisdom: writing your first draft commits you to nothing. Everything is still up for grabs, even when your draft is the 365-page chunk of text that your year's investment of lunch-break scribbling has produced. You can buy The Voice off with this truth: maybe the sentence you just wrote *is* rubbish. If it is, it doesn't matter, because you'll catch it on the second pass, when you are revising what you have written. Because 'writing' is a two-part process; and that two-part combines bronze and silver rules in one central truth:

First you get it written; then *you get it right.*

The beauty of this slogan is not only that it frees you from the imaginary tentacles of 'writer's block'; it is that when you do go back to revise what you have previously written you discover, eight times out of ten, that the sentence you thought so hideous is actually fine. Actually works pretty well. Is actually pretty exciting.

Writers all share this one truth (that they write) – but they find a glorious diversity of ways of actualizing it. Some like to plan carefully, with plot trees, chapter summaries and character thumbnails. And that's fine so long as the planning doesn't supplant the actual writing. Others like to hurl themselves into the fray and just start writing, and leave the structuring and plotting and polishing to the revision period. Speaking for myself, I tread a middle path, although it meanders closer to the latter rather than the former. This is what I do: I have a sense of where the story starts, I know where I want it to end up, and I know the key scenes or high points I want to hit on the way. Then I sit down and start writing. The idea is to strike a balance between, on the one hand, over-preparing my ground – which can so easily give an arid over-masticated texture to the final product – and, on the other, just splurging any old thing – which can result in a chaos too formless to shape during revision. I tend to find that writing this way gives me enough of the pleasures of finding out where the story is going as I proceed that I don't become bored, but enough structure to keep the whole thing in view.

And finishing what you write is how we separate out the dilettantes from the pros. For a long time as a young writer I would start writing a novel, only to abandon it after a hundred pages, or a chapter, or even a couple of pages. The idea would be bright and enticing in my head, and I would start writing. Then at some point (and this is inevitable, believe me) a sense of weariness and failure would start to nag at me. It wasn't working. It wasn't capturing what was so cool about the idea. I should give up and try again with this other idea I just had! And so the cycle would begin again. I didn't start becoming a proper writer until I grasped that I had to push through to the end of my initial idea, no matter how bad or hopeless I considered it while it was going on.

You must revise what you write

I've already mentioned this a few times but I'm going to say more about it here. In the movie *Amadeus*, Mozart composes flawless music direct on to the staves. But I am not Mozart; and I seriously doubt whether you are either. If you find yourself reluctant to revise, take a long hard look. Is it that you think, 'Oh, lordy, I'm too embarrassed to re-read what I've written. I'll just chuck this out to a publisher, cross my fingers and hope it's okay.' That won't cut it. Perhaps you think, 'My job is to get the ideas out there, in however rough a form; publishers have editors to get all the fiddly grammatical and stylistic points right ...' If that's what you think, then you are wrong!

Revising your prose is as central to 'writing' as putting down a first draft.

There's a particular reason why the silver rule stands higher on my metaphorical medals podium than the bronze rule. It is because the process of revising turns you into a reader again. This is worth dwelling upon, actually, because there are dangers as well as glories in conceiving of yourself as 'a writer' (up there with Tolstoy, J.K. Rowling and your favourite author). Not least among these is the vainglory of actually writing something. I'm not snarking when I say this. I've been a published writer for many years, but I'm still subject to this little spurt of self-regard when I finish a novel ... because, hey, writing novels is really hard and, despite that fact, I did it! It's fine to take pride in your work, and being able to finish a novel is indeed an accomplishment, a victory over the day-job deadline and the pram in the hall, a series of smaller victories over time-poverty, exhaustion, discouragement, illness and self-doubt.

Finishing your novel meant triumphing over many hardships and obstacles. I congratulate you! I do so honestly, with (as the phrase goes) a laurel – and a hearty handshake. I do so because I have been there with you, in the trenches. I know how hard it can be. Just getting to the end of the process of writing is a signal achievement. But I also have to tell you this: the reader doesn't care. She has no interest in what obstacles you overcame to write the book. She doesn't care about your time pressures, your bouts of depression, the knockbacks and rejection letters you had to steel yourself to get past. The reader only cares about one thing: is this book any good? And that's what you owe the reader: that your short story or novel be good.

The converse is also true, actually. The reader is not impressed that you managed to bang out this whole 90,000-word space opera in only three weeks ('I was on a roll! I hardly slept!') – the reader only cares whether your 90,000-word space opera is any good. It is no use addressing your imaginary reader with 'Hey, maybe my book isn't perfect, but you gotta understand the trials and tribulations I underwent writing it ...' Your girlfriend or boyfriend might conceivably care about that. Your friends may care. Your mother should care. But your readers have no obligation to forgive shoddy work because you happened to be going through a tough time writing it.

Not that you will produce shoddy work, of course. You have too much self-respect, and respect for the craft, to do that. But the glamour of actually writing something can dazzle even the most discriminating writer. Me, I comprehend how impressive it is that you finally finished your story. Bravo! But the reader is going to take that for granted. She will not say, 'Well, it's not very good, but the fact that the author managed to get it written at all is an achievement! So I'm going to cut the work some slack.'

Revising is the time you turn yourself into a reader of your own stuff. Rewriting is a kind of reading. It may be that you need to give yourself a suitable length of time between composing the work and revising the work in order to be able to see what you have done with a reader's eye: days, or weeks, or (if you can spare the time) longer still.

Here's the good news: we are all readers first, and therefore foremost. We all read before we started writing; so we can all return to that state to revise our own writing.

What do I mean by 'revising'? Well, in part I mean the obvious: spotting typos, grammatical solecisms and clumsinesses of expression; recasting clichés, eliminating inelegant repetitions and deleting that section when you fell droolingly asleep on the keyboard and inadvertently typed the phrase *&^XSDW??ER21"$* over and over again. That's all (certainly) part of it. But there are more important things revising should do.

Samuel Delany

'I'm a very bad writer. What I am is a good rewriter.'

Writing is slow. More specifically, writing is slower than reading. It may take you half a day to write a thousand words; but even quite a slow reader can read thousand words in a quarter of an hour. And this is one of the central problems any writer faces: knowing how to scale their writing up from the pace at which it gets written to the pace at which it gets read. There is an added complication: different readers read at different rates. Some rattle through whole novels in an afternoon; others carefully and scrupulously follow the sentence thread over many weeks. Yet your job, as writer, is to construct your work so that the readers hit the beats they need to hit for the story to work.

It's not often discussed in writing manuals, but actually this is one of the most intractable technical problems a writer faces. I have nothing but respect for authors who are very good at it – Stephen King, for example, possesses an almost superhuman ability to time and pace his narratives; to know how long to draw out the tension, to know exactly where to place the shocks and bombshells. How does he do it? How can you do it? Only by going through your own work as a reader, surrendering yourself to its tempo. To do this, you need to disengage your writerly mechanism, slip the clutch on your *amour-propre* and forget where you were and what you were thinking when you penned it. You need to imagine you're encountering it for the first time.

Revising is correcting the specific copy-text, either by actually changing what you have written or else (and this is just as valid a strategy) marking text as 'not quite right' and coming back to it later. But revising is also acquiring a sense of how well timed the plotting is; of how believable the characters are; of whether the dialogue has the snap and verve of actual speech or (too often in genre) has only the grey drone of characters infodumping mercilessly upon one another. Revising is when you get a feel for your piece.

 ## Key idea

'Novum' is the word coined by SF critic Darko Suvin to differentiate the SF story from other kinds of story. It means 'new thing', the thing that the SF story has that is not *in* the real world. A story with no 'novum' is just a regular story. The novum might be a piece of kit (starship, robot, time machine or so on); or something less concrete – Le Guin's *Left Hand of Darkness* is based on the 'novum' of a society in which gender is not 'fixed' as it is in our world, such that everybody has periods as both a man and a woman. A short road to a good SF story is to make your novum both original and resonant – not just to recycle the starships, robots and time machines of a thousand earlier SF stories, but to come up with something more striking.

Show, don't tell

Is that *really* the golden rule? Didn't I just say, earlier, that one business of the writer was to wage war on cliché – and isn't this the hoariest 'how to write' cliché of them all? What does it even mean? Surely a storyteller *tells a story* … it's right there in the name! What's wrong with telling?

Give me a moment and I'll show you.

It is a commonplace of books like this to say, in one way or another, 'rules are there to be broken'. That's a slightly puzzling phrase, actually. Clearly some rules – let's say, rules concerning murder, robbery and the conspiracy to pervert the course of justice, are very much *not* there to be broken. Even in a writing context, there are many rules that you should strive earnestly and with all your heart to uphold, including the rules of basic grammar. The justification for it is the notion that the author who slavishly follows the rules can produce only hack-work, whereas the true literary genius treats so-called 'rules' with gay, James-Joyce-ish abandon.

I think the mistake comes from rolling together two senses of what we mean by 'rules'. I am not trying to be prescriptive or (worse) authoritarian in this book. The path to being a good writer is not the slavish internalization of a set of rigid 'thou shalt not' commandments. As a matter of personal philosophy, I consider it the business of the artist to follow the wise words of a recent contemporary poet and *fight* the power, *fight* the powers that be (you got to, etc.).

There's another sense in which the word 'rules' is relevant here. This is rules as form. Rules structure our experience of the text. You can play various formal and structural games with your writing; but completely formless or structure-free writing isn't avant-garde or envelope-pushing: it's a mess. And, above all, you must avoid making a mess. Mess is not the index of aesthetic sprawl; it is an index to a failure of ambition.

This is doubly applicable to science fiction. Science fiction is a genre, and genres are determined by 'rules' or 'forms'. If you blindly reproduce these forms, it's likely your story of a singing spaceship, a friendly alien visitor or a Pinocchioesque robot will seem merely stale and over-familiar. But by the same token, you cannot simply sweep away all these forms and hope still to write science fiction.

'Show, don't tell' is not a rule to be followed, so much as it is a discipline to which you should apply yourself; and the point of that discipline is to prevent yourself from writing in a lazy or merely formulaic way. In that sense it is a kind of anti-rule, or at least a means by which you can avoid being trapped by too-strong conventional elements.

Keeping 'show, don't tell' in view is a way of pushing yourself to think harder about how to present your cool SF idea or neat SF prop; and that means it is a way of helping you write more interesting, engaging and elegant prose.

Key idea

I'll give you an example of what I mean. If you are writing a story about adultery in Hampstead or robbery in Chicago, you can take it for granted that your readers have a pretty good sense of what Hampstead or Chicago are like. You can sketch your setting; no need to layer it stodgily on with a trowel. But science fiction is trickier, because you can't be sure your readers know what Frolix 9 or The Ultramatrix look like. And in that situation the temptation is – to tell them.

Resist that temptation.

Here's one form of 'telling, not showing', from my ongoing and totally imaginary Space Opera Magnum Opus *Captain Diehard and the Comet Chameleons*:

> *Jamie Church settled into his Captain's chair on the Bridge of USS the* Megasaucer *and addressed himself to his second in command.*
>
> *'As you know, Bob, Einstein's laws make it impossible to travel faster than light. In order to get round this difficulty, our spaceship generates a warp-bubble in spacetime, which is then directed towards the stars by means of superquantum directed vibranticules. Theoretically, once within the superquantum bubble we should be immune to attack.'*
>
> *'And yet the Spectre Aliens were able to fire a de-integrator beam directly through our hull!' exclaimed Number Two.*
>
> *'Indeed they did. Which means they must have found a way precisely to match* their *directed vibranticules with ours. And to do that, someone must have given them access to our navigation codes. Somebody ...' Abruptly he leapt to his feet, holding out his arm in accusation.*
> *'... on this bridge!'*

This gets key information across to the reader, but does so in way that is both inelegant and clogging. Compare this paragraph from the equally made-up and imaginary novelization *The Fast and the Furious 13: Green Ideas Sleep Furiously*, set not in the SF future but in the realistic present-day:

> 'Dirk –' Bob expostulated. 'We'll never get there on time! It's right on the other side of town!'
>
> 'Normally you'd be right,' said Dirk, through clenched teeth. 'It would take hours to walk the distance. But I have a car! And as you know, such a vehicle operates according to the principle of internal combustion, where a series of controlled mini-explosions created by releasing and igniting a succession of small amounts of petroleum in a specially designed chamber drives pistons that in turn turn the driveshaft and so the wheels. It sounds cumbersome, but in practice the motor runs so rapidly and smoothly that the vehicle can be propelled at speeds in excess of a hundred miles an hour. We can be there in minutes ...'

That's not a fair comparison, of course. As a writer you can take it for granted that your reader knows how an automobile works, whereas you can't take it for granted she knows how a warp drive works. The challenge, though, is to find a way of conveying the salient points of your SF novum that is graceful, elegant, amusing, cool and never dully informative.

Infodumping insults the reader. Worse than that (much worse!) it *bores* the reader. In effect, it says: 'In order to understand my story, you need to understand a few things about my invented world, and here is a mini lecture to get you up to speed ...'

The way to avoid infodumping is already to be up to speed. Since I earlier perpetrated one 'how to' writing guide cliché ('Show, don't tell'), I feel ready to drop another on you. It's this one: less is more. What that means is that the less you tell the reader about your ingenious spaceship drive, the specific design of your robot or the layout of your future city, the more she has to fill in for herself. That 'filling-in' is called imaginative engagement, and the best reading experiences are the ones where we readers are imaginatively drawn into the world of the book.

Common sense tells us that 'less is more' only goes so far – extrapolate it to its logical conclusion and we'd have 'nothing is everything!' which is clearly nonsense. (If that were true, then bookshops would sell books full of empty pages to which readers would then apply their imaginations to create worlds of marvel. Bookshops could sell 'imaginative marvel seeds' along with their books. Readers would swallow these and begin the writing. Actually, that's not a bad starting point for a fantasy story …)

Snapshot exercise

Write an account of one of the following things as if you were a Martian author, writing for other Martians who had never come across them before. Spend no more than five minutes doing this, but ensure that you let your imaginary readers know all the crucial elements – what they are, how they work and how it is that human beings are so attached to them:

- a coffee machine
- a pogo stick
- an electric nose-hair trimmer
- a woman taking her dog for a walk
- a man using Twitter to tell the world that he has just eaten a biscuit.

The real challenge now (should you wish to accept it) is to rewrite your description so that it no longer infodumps upon the reader but in a way that would still make sense to a Martian who has never encountered the item before.

You need to give your readers' imagination something to chew upon. The point is that you should take care not to stuff their craws with great quantities of fact. You want to suggest, not exhaustively explain, your world. It's not only more elegant, it's more effective. You could spend a whole page detailing every futuristic gizmo and prop in your character's twenty-second-century living space, which would certainly get across to your reader that the story is set in a future world. But you can do the same thing in a sentence that describes the character leaving the apartment with the phrase 'the door dilated'. That happens to be a phrase famous in SF circles, from golden-age SF writer Robert Heinlein. There's a reason fans love it: it finesses the need to establish the future setting without holding the reader up.

Now it may be that there are elements of your SF universe that you have to explain in greater detail. For instance, you may have to give specific details that are vital for your story, or lay out something for the reader that they will need to know if they're to understand the rest of the story.

If so, then keep 'show, don't tell' in view: aim for elegance rather than the clumping foot of over-explication; try to pare away all the stuff that you don't need until you're left with just enough to put your point across. Keep it natural.

Instead of describing your futuristic device, talk about the ways it works or, better still, the ways it doesn't. The person on the car's passenger seat today would never turn to the driver and ask, 'How does this car we're travelling in *work*, then, Bob?' – but they might well ask, 'What's that weird knocking noise in the engine?' – and that question can be enough to enable you to let the reader know how the engine works without lecturing them.

Key idea

Award-winning SF author Jo Walton has coined the word 'incluing' to describe how she puts her stories together; and she has some characteristically wise words about the practice:

'Incluing is the process of scattering information seamlessly through the text, as opposed to stopping the story to impart the information. Incluing is anything where you provide the information through clues and implication rather than infodumps. And you can inclue everything, though background is the easiest to talk about – you can inclue character development and plot. "The door dilated" (Heinlein, *Beyond this Horizon*) is incluing. Stopping the story for an infodump about how traffic lights work and how amazing this is (Heinlein, *Job*) is incluing about how the person doing this comes from a world without them. It's just plain more interesting to read about the shadows growing more purple as the red sun sets, and then later have someone out early seeing the blue sun rise, than to start off with the astronomy of binary stars – even if you do want to get into that, getting into it when the reader already cares about the shadows is better.'

Try to fold your infodump discreetly into some other piece of crucial storytelling. If your future world is one in which people have genetically engineered their hair to work like fish gills, filtering oxygen directly into the bloodstream so that they can live under water without cumbersome breathing apparatus, don't start your story with 'In the twenty-fourth century scientists had found a way of genetically engineering human hair to work like fish gills, filtering oxygen directly into the bloodstream so that people can live under water without the need for cumbersome breathing apparatus ...' And don't have one character say to another, 'Do you know what, Bob? I'm real glad science found a way of genetically engineering our hair to work like fish gills, filtering oxygen directly into the bloodstream so that we're able to live under water without needing cumbersome breathing apparatus, since it has opened up whole tracts of the seabed for human habitation, easing the pressure on our over-populated Earth ...' Instead, start telling your story, telling just enough to show that it's set under water. Then, once the character dynamics and the storytelling have started building up momentum, work your infodump slyly into some more important feature of the tale. Maybe it's central to your story that your main character is depressed, or heartbroken, or ill – so have him neglect his personal hygiene with the effect that an algae growth builds up on his hair, interfering with his ability to 'breathe' under water. Maybe he has to be hospitalized, or taken to the surface. Have one character murder another by cutting off his hair. If you're feeling bolder, only hint at the hair thing, with a few choice descriptions of the fronds of your main character's splendid mullet, drifting through the oxygen-rich waters. See how far you can take it before the reader starts to think 'Wait a minute, how are these people able to walk about on the sea bed without drowning ...?'

The general rule of thumb is: you convey much more with the form and style of your writing than your content. If your characters are twenty-second-century Venusians, it's a poor idea to have them walk around and talk like 1950s Londoners. They need to walk and talk like twenty-second-century Venusians; and if they do that, then you hardly need to add external description of them at all.

Context is also your friend. Readers are clever, and they pick up more than you think.

Workshop 1

Here is a story I wrote a few years ago in part as an exercise in finishing a story in 100 words (because my stories tend to go on and on ...); it was republished in my 2013 short story collection *Adam Robots*. Do you see what I did there, with the title to that collection?

The Cow

The cow jumped over the moon. The cow jumped under the moon. The cow went around and around the moon. The cow, altering its course fractionally, spiralled in and landed upon the moon. The cow docked. The cow vented four hundred thousand litres of milk into the lunar refectory reservoir. The cow was made of a mixture of metal and plastic. The cow refuelled. The cow decoupled. The cow was piloted by an AI with an equivalent 30% more-than-bovine mental capacity. The cow jumped to orbit again.

Dawg, watching from Alpha's main observatory, sucked on a stimulant delivery package. The stimulant filled him with pleasurable thoughts.

In order to write a story in only 100 words I had to rely upon the reader being able to apply a larger context to my words. How much work can such context do before the reader loses her bearings?

Is the character 'Dawg' a tall man or a short man? Yes, I know the story doesn't specifically *tell* you how tall he is; but you can answer the question anyway. In some way the story manages to *show* you his height.

Does this story seem to you complete in itself, or does it need to be developed further? If you had to carry the story on, what would you do? (Hint: what science-fictional dish? What science-fictional spoon?)

Workshop 2

Look again at the five-minute microstory that you wrote earlier, the one beginning with the sentence 'When the news announced the end of the world that morning, Jay ...'

What would you change about it now?

Does it need continuing? If so, how would you develop the idea? If not – congratulations! You wrote a whole story.

Write a short story

Write a version of the story of 'Little Red Riding Hood' in which the wolf is an alien. This story should be complete in 750 words or fewer, and you are free to reinterpret the original fairy tale any way you wish: set it in the past, the present or the future; set it on Earth or on another world; make the alien a shape-shifter, a bug-blattered-beast monster or something more uncanny; resolve the story any way you like. But do not 'infodump' your account of the alien, or the world through which your 'Red' moves.

In keeping with the points discussed in this chapter, set yourself a time limit – say, two hours. Write a first draft without pausing over the individual sentences or fretting too much. Then put it aside and come back to it the following day.

Summary

The three rules of writing – write, revise and show, don't tell – are offered here as a metaphorical cornerstone to the construction of your writing shack. The rest of the chapter elaborates on these three items. I stand by my insistence that there is no such thing as writer's block – since the block is a metaphorical state rather than an actual one, it stands to reason that it can be metaphorically banished. Less dogmatic is the insistence that writing and revising are two separate processes; they are for this author, but you may find other strategies. As long as you do find workable strategies, it hardly matters what they are. Infodumping, though, is clearly a bad thing and needs to be minimized.

Where to next?

In the next chapter we will get a sense of what science fiction and fantasy actually are.

2

What are science fiction and fantasy? (And what does that mean about how you write them?)

The point of this chapter is not to fight through the tedious arguments about the academic 'definitions' of science fiction and fantasy. It is to talk through a sense of genre as a practical guide, to help you.

During the course of this chapter we will work through some of the (very) many subgenres of science fiction and fantasy, consider the advantages and disadvantages of positioning yourself generically and discuss how to gauge the appropriate level of research for your chosen subgenre. Then we will go on to sketch out accounts of 'hard SF', 'soft SF', 'heroic fantasy' and the anti-Tolkien, or Grimdark, fantastical traditions.

'Genre' is the French word for a 'type' or 'sort' of thing. In general discourse today it is often used to distinguish between high and popular culture – between the 'literary' novel on the one hand, and the 'genre' output of writers of crime, chicklit, horror, historical, thriller, fantasy and SF novels on the other. I've never liked this usage, if I'm honest – party because the 'literary' novel (the sort of book that might win the Pulitzer or Booker Prize) is also a genre, but mostly because the literary history of the last 30 years has been one of (to use critic Gary Wolfe's phrase) the 'evaporation' of genres. Pulitzer Prize winning novels like Jennifer Egan's *A Visit from the Goon Squad* (2010), or Booker winners like Eleanor Catton's *The Luminaries* (2013), draw deeply on the tropes of science fiction and the fantastic.

There's another point: to think in terms of genres is to undertake the pigeonholing of literature. It means bundling together various books that may be in other respects completely different from one another and slotting them all into categories marked things like 'defeating the monster', 'time travel' or 'alien invasion'. The film based on the Old English epic *Beowulf* and the 1982 movie *The Terminator* are both about defeating a monster, yet these two films are as different from one another as could be imagined. Wells's *The Time Machine* is a time-travel story; so is Proust's *A la recherche du temps perdu*. You take my point. Do not let your writing be wholly defined by its genre label. Pigeonholes are graves.

That said (that wrenching noise you can hear is me applying the handbrake to execute a rapid turn), you need to be aware of the way genre works if you want to be a writer. Practically speaking, it's how publishers work; and the reason it is how publishers work is that it is how readers think. Your job is to surprise readers without alienating them entirely; and to know that, you need to know what readers are used to.

Science fiction is not 'a genre'; fantasy is not 'another genre'. They are both collections of subgenres, related families of writing types that get lumped together by marketing people and booksellers.

This chapter is going to step briskly through the varieties of science fiction and fantasy, with hints, tips and exercises on how to write each of them. There's a wild-card entry, too, for both science fiction and fantasy. These lists don't pretend to be entirely exhaustive, either. One of the beauties of genre writing is the potential it offers to mash-up and creative rejigging. Science fiction gives you the chance not only to invent cool new concepts, imagine new technologies and new models for life – it also gives you the chance to invent brand-new genres. Why not be the first to write an Eggpunk story? There's been a wealth of science fiction written based on extrapolating ideas from physics, biology and chemistry – why don't you try extrapolating ideas from logic, systems theory or logical positivism?

Before we get to the subgenres, though, there's another angle to genre that you'll need to factor in. In ancient Greek critical writing, 'genre' meant something more to do with the tone of stories than their content. Aristotle distinguished between four genres: tragedy, epic, comedy and parody. He had a little scheme that he used to derive these labels – one the one hand he thought literature could either be 'superior' (elevating and noble) or 'inferior' (appealing to our baser appetites for laughter and fun). He also separated out 'dramatic' from 'narrative'; the former is basically people talking to one another, the latter is stuff happening. Parse these four possibles against one another and you have:

- Tragedy – superior, dramatic.
- Epic – superior, narrative.
- Comedy – inferior, dramatic.
- Parody – inferior, narrative.

The distinction between 'comic' and 'tragic' still has purchase today, although because you will be almost certainly writing in the novel and short story tradition, and because the novel is for historical reasons basically a comic mode (that's a large claim, I know; and I don't have time to develop it here), you will find it hard writing 'pure' high seriousness. You are, of course, welcome to try, just as you are welcome to write outside the short-story/novel paradigm if you like. For myself, I'm always fascinated to see science-fictional epic poetry, science-fictional tragic drama, science-fictional lyric poems and the like.

The thing is, writing 'comedy' does not mean writing gags and punchlines. It means writing human warmth and a degree of sweetness. And such qualities are not incompatible with tragedy – quite the reverse. A comic mode can feed the pathos and emotional potency of tragedy in a way that writing that is too serious and po-faced simply cannot.

There's one term that Aristotle himself admits is missing from his list – lyric. It's missing because Aristotle believed that art should reflect life, it should 'be about' things and the things it was about should be recognizably the things of actual life. He called this 'mimesis', the Greek word behind the English words 'imitation', 'mimic' and so on. Lyric poetry was just beautiful, and might not be about anything other than its own loveliness.

These Aristotelian terms have a different set of meanings for the twenty-first-century reader, of course; but these meanings still owe something to their conceptual etymology, and have specific relevance to the writing of science fiction and fantasy:

- Tragedy – it ends sadly.
- Epic – it is really long.
- Comedy – it makes you laugh.
- Parody – it imitates a famous original in mockingly deflating fashion.

'Genre' is the elevation of 'convention' to a structuring principle. Thinking in terms of subgeneric categories can be a useful exercise in terms of orienting yourself with respect to what you want to do – even if it is just (as it is with me) the nerdy completist's desire to write at least one story in every recognized category. But this doesn't mean that you should allow your imagination to be trammeled by generic conventions. Remember: wage space-war on cliché.

 ## Snapshot exercise

Here is a list of a variety of subgenres generally associated with the 'fantastic' or the 'science-fictional'. Which subgenres are missing from this list?

Pick, and rank, the three subgenres you would most like to write.

- Time travel
- Interplanetary adventure
- Alternative history
- Military science fiction
- Climate change
- Zombies/Vampires/Monsters
- Robots

- Golden age
- Cyberpunk
- Medieval fantasy
- Non-European fantasy
- Steampunk
- Magical realism

The origins of science fiction

Key idea: Hugo Gernsback

Hugo Gernsback (1884–1967) was a Luxembourger who emigrated to the United States in 1904. He has a special place in the traditions of science fiction because in 1926 he founded the first magazine dedicated to the genre, *Amazing Stories* (the magazine was published through to 2005; after a hiatus it is now available as an online journal). He claimed that his idea of a perfect SF story was '75% literature interwoven with 25% science'.

Some critics think science fiction begins when the term itself was first used – by Hugo Gernsback in the 1920s. Others point out that books by H.G. Wells and Jules Verne published in the nineteenth century are clearly 'science fiction' in all but name, and date the genre to that epoch as a reaction to the sudden and world-changing advances in technology and science that characterized the Victorian phase of the Industrial Revolution. Myself, I date the beginning of the genre earlier. I go all the way back to the 1600s, and Johannes Kepler, whose *Somnium* (written perhaps as early as 1600, although not published until 1632) brings the best scientific and astronomical knowledge of the day to bear on the question of imagining what lunar aliens might actually look like. There are other critics again who think we might as well bracket Lucian's sailing-ship-swept-up-in-a-storm-and-set-down-on-the-moon *True History* (first century CE) or, indeed, Homer's Cyclops and the monsters from the Epic of Gilgamesh as 'science fiction'.

Does this historical narrative matter? These different historical accounts of the genre actually put in place four different senses of what the genre is.

 Focus point

Which of the four start points above seems to you the one that describes the origin point of 'science fiction' best?

a You think 'science fiction' begins in 1926. This means you think of science fiction as something relatively young, something distinctively modern and contemporary – a literature that responds to the now.

b If you think science fiction begins in the Victorian epoch, you think of it as to do with a longer historical narrative, emerging from the era of the first heavy industry of the Industrial Revolution, from the Age of Empires and the high-water mark of European Realist fiction.

c If you think science fiction is as old as literature, then you think of it as a fundamentally mythic mode of art, one that touches on ancient archetypes of human fascination and endeavour – the voyage of exploration, the fight with monsters, death and transcendence. 'Technology' is as old as humanity, after all – man is the tool-making animal – and science fiction can engage with technology in myriad ways.

Workshop

Imagine a story of aliens invading the Earth. Sketch out how you would tell this story:

a set today

b if it happened in 1848

c if it happened during the Peloponnesian Wars.

Think about not only how these different situations alter the circumstances of the tale, but also the way you tell it.

Hard science fiction

Key idea

Hard science fiction is characterized by its commitment to the accuracy of its scientific and technical detail. It was first used, approvingly, in a review of John W. Campbell's 1957 novel *Islands of Space*, and remains a popular flavour of the science-fictional. Hard scence fiction is happiest portraying worlds where rules can be crisply identified and where following such rules is rewarded: its heroes may be scientists, explorers or members of the military. 'Military science fiction', though it often plays fast and loose with the realities of science, is often seen as a subset of hard science fiction.

Since 'accuracy' is the shibboleth for many fans of this stuff, and since the Internet has made checking facts – and communicating one's dissatisfaction to the author – easier than used to be the case, if writing hard science fiction is your dream, you will need to do more research for your story than you would for other kinds of writing.

A scientific education helps; but a greater help is a willingness to do some intellectual legwork. There are a great many excellent books and articles about science written with the general reader in mind; and Wikipedia is full of wonders if searched carefully. Subscribe to the *New Scientist*. Keep up to date with the latest science news. More helpful still are scientifically knowledgeable friends past whom you can run your ideas to check their plausibility. Search online for 'hard sf writers' groups' and request, courteously, to join. If you do so, then do so in good faith: be prepared to put in the time and effort helping the others in the group perfect their writing; don't just go in to help yourself to others' points of view and then scarper.

And writing proper hard science fiction strikes at the imaginative freedom that powers much fantastic writing generally. You know the score; you're too canny to have your spaceship's laser cannons making a noise in the vacuum of space; you know about such things.

Here are some tenets of actual science that most science fiction routinely contradicts. In each case, take a popular SF text (*Star Wars*, *Star Trek*, *Doctor Who*, whatever you are most familiar with) and determine how the work would have to be changed if actual science were observed.

- Faster-than-light travel
- Matter transportation
- Tractor 'beams'
- Anti-gravity and/or artificial gravity
- Regeneration.

There's a second kind of research you may need to undertake, depending on how much of a fan of this stuff you already are. One thing no writer can afford to do is to reinvent the wheel – the more you read around the backlist of science fiction, the better placed you'll be to develop your own idea in an original manner.

Here are some 'classic' hard SF stories and novels. You'll note that most of these are written by men – not a recommendation, of course, but indicative of what used to be the cultural bias of this kind of writing. It's much less true (though it probably is truer of hard science fiction than it used to be: there are men who can make a fetish out of 'hardness') that this is a boy's-only club: but if you want to write this kind of thing you could do worse than challenging the assumptions behind this. Few things are as backward-looking and therefore so out of place in a forward-looking mode like science fiction as 'sexism'.

SHORT STORIES
- Hal Clement, 'Uncommon Sense' (1945)
- James Blish, 'Surface Tension' (1952)
- Tom Godwin, 'The Cold Equations' (1954)
- Poul Anderson, 'Kyrie' (1968)
- Frederik Pohl, 'Day Million' (1971)
- Larry Niven, 'Inconstant Moon' (1971), 'The Hole Man' (1974)

- Greg Bear, 'Tangents' (1986)
- Geoffrey A. Landis, 'A Walk in the Sun' (1991)

NOVELS
- Hal Clement, *Mission of Gravity* (1953)
- Arthur C. Clarke, *A Fall of Moondust* (1961), *Rendezvous with Rama* (1972)
- Poul Anderson, *Tau Zero* (1970)
- Robert L. Forward, *Dragon's Egg* (1980)
- A.K. Dewdney, *The Planiverse* (1984)
- Stephen Baxter, *Ring* (1996)
- Charles Sheffield, *Between the Strokes of Night* (1985)
- Kim Stanley Robinson, the 'Mars' trilogy: *Red Mars* (1992); *Green Mars* (1993); *Blue Mars* (1996)
- Nancy Kress, *Beggars in Spain* (1993)
- Greg Egan, *Schild's Ladder* (2002)
- Alastair Reynolds, *Pushing Ice* (2005)
- Paul J. McAuley, *The Quiet War* (2008)

Soft science fiction

I can't say I like the tag 'soft', here, although I've rather backed myself into a corner by starting with 'hard' science fiction. So let me be clear: I don't call this second variety of science fiction 'soft' in order to impugn the rigour with which it is worked through, or the power and force of which it is capable. Far from it.

More to the point, you won't find two critics ready to agree on what the boundaries between 'hard' and 'soft' even are. For some, science fiction that deviates in any way whatsoever from the 'rules' of science is soft science fiction. For others, some scientific impossibilities – faster-than-light travel, telepathy – can be included in a hard SF story without compromising its 'hardness'; and soft science fiction means writing that depends, in effect, upon magic – 'science fantasy' is a label sometimes applied.

For others – and I include myself in this group – too vehement an insistence on the rhetoric of 'hardness' is a suspect proxy for masculine phallic boasting. Science fiction is not only an exploration of 'science'; it is also a metaphorical mode of art that aims to represent the world without reproducing it. The limitation in much hard-SF writing is too myopic a focus on the technical and engineering details of the story. For instance, in Stanislaw Lem's brilliant *Solaris* (1961) – a novel I have sometimes seen described as hard science fiction – astronauts discover an ocean planet which appears, as the novel goes on, to be a single vast sentient life form capable of creating material 'ghosts' drawn from the crew's memory. Lem gives us no notion as to how the spaceship arrived at the Planet Solaris – faster than light travel? slower? – or the precise mechanism by which the planet is able to read and interpret the minds of the human crew. This isn't because Lem was scientifically incompetent (in fact, he was unusually well and widely read in modern discourses of science). It is because he's not interested in those aspects of his story. *Solaris* the novel is not about interstellar space travel; it is about memory and loss, about encountering radical otherness and the danger that such an encounter would resolve into a solipsistic reaffirmation of the human. And this is the point: writing this story by giving over a large proportion of the narrative to the technical exigencies of the spacecraft and so on would be to diminish the resonance of those central conceits.

Soft science fiction is more likely to place an emphasis on character or society – on the psychology of space travel as much as the mechanics of it. It may extrapolate story ideas from the 'soft sciences': anthropology, ecology, economics, evolution, futures studies, intelligence, linguistics, perception, psychology and sociology. Indeed, there is a whole gold mine's worth of new ideas waiting to be excavated from those disciplines in a way that simply isn't true of 'physics' and 'chemistry'.

Some people prefer the label 'speculative fiction' to 'science fiction' in order precisely to downplay the 'scientific' expectations of the readership (without sacrificing those well-known initials, 'SF'). 'Imaginative literature', 'Fantastika', 'The Weird' and other descriptors are sometimes applied.

Karel Čapek's stage play *R.U.R.* (1921) is the work that gave us the word 'robot' – the initials of its title stand for 'Rossum's Universal Robots', after the factory owner whose facility produces the artificial humanoids. But Čapek has no interest in the practical or technical aspects of how his robots have been manufactured. He is interested only in the social implications of this new and unlimited supply of artificial workers.

Ursula Le Guin's *The Left Hand of Darkness* (1968) – one of my very favourite of all SF novels, actually – is set on a distant snowbound planet called Winter. Here, gender is not fixed as it mostly is on Earth; instead the humanoid inhabitants are gender neutral for most of the time, and become male or female only when on heat (in 'kemmer', as Le Guin puts it). Individuals may become either male or female, and experience existence as both over the course of their lives, capable of being both fathers and mothers. Le Guin works out her worldbuilding with commendable care and consistency, but this is not a 'hard' SF novel – and not only because it includes mystic and telepathic elements. It is because the book's main focus is to imagine how society might work without the implicit symbolic structuring principle of 'male' and 'female' that is so powerfully at work in our actual Earth societies.

William Gibson's *Neuromancer* (1984) is the novel that, more than any other, kick-started and defined 'Cyberpunk'. Its account of a futuristic computer hacker entering the shared virtual reality of The Matrix (Gibson's influential coinage) and having a series of noir-style adventures remains compelling reading. But Gibson had no actual knowledge of computer programming or the scientific logics of programming. Instead he was inspired by watching his kids playing video games.

A list of the greatest SF ever written will, it seems to me, lean heavily on 'speculative' or 'soft' SF:

- Jonathan Swift, *Gulliver's Travels* (1726)
- Aldous Huxley, *Brave New World* (1932)
- George Orwell, *Nineteen Eighty-Four* (1949)
- Philip K. Dick, *The Man in the High Castle* (1962); *The Three Stigmata of Palmer Eldritch* (1965); *Do Androids Dream of Electric Sheep?* (1968); *Ubik* (1969)
- Frank Herbert, *Dune* (1965)
- Samuel Delany, *Babel-17* (1966)
- J.G. Ballard, *The Crystal World* (1966)
- Jack Vance, *Emphyrio* (1969)
- Ursula Le Guin, *The Dispossessed: An Ambiguous Utopia* (1974)
- Gene Wolfe, *The Fifth Head of Cerberus* (1972)

- Octavia Butler, *Kindred* (1979)
- Margaret Atwood, *The Handmaid's Tale* (1986); *Oryx and Crake* (2003)
- Sheri Tepper, *Grass* (1989)
- China Miéville, *Perdido Street Station* (2000)
- Geoff Ryman, *Air* (2005)
- Kazuo Ishiguro, *Never Let Me Go* (2006)
- Francis Spufford, *Red Plenty* (2010)
- Kameron Hurley, *God's War* (2010). I include this splendid novel to make the point that soft science fiction can be, as this novel is, bone-jarringly hard in the way it tells its story.

Fantasy

In one sense, fantasy is the oldest kind of literature we have. The oldest surviving examples of literature – the Sumerian *Epic of Gilgamesh*, Homer's *Iliad* and *Odyssey*, the folk stories from Africa and the Far East – all include 'fantastic' elements: gods and monsters, magic spells and prophecies, charmed weapons and talking animals. The fantastic is the default mode of human storytelling. This makes sense when you think about it: people don't need stories of actual life. They are, all of them, living natural life. They are bound to be more interested in the unfamiliar than the familiar.

We, though, happen to live at a time when this dominance has been – temporarily – challenged. In the eighteenth century a new kind of story emerged: narratives of domestic interaction and courtship that worked according to a logic of 'plausibility'. In the nineteenth century this became a cultural dominant in Europe and America: 'realism'. For reasons I've never entirely understood, this desire to 'hold as 'twere the mirror up to nature' (ah, Shakespeare!) became associated with the 'High' Modernist literary experiments of the early twentieth century, leaving fantastic stories of heroic barbarian warriors and silver spire-shaped interplanetary rockets to the Pulp tradition of 'Low' populism. There's nothing intrinsically 'High' about realism, it seems to me (on the contrary, in fact). Still, that's where we are. For many people, 'realism' is reputable and serious; 'fantasy' is disreputable and frivolous.

I rehearse this because it is good to be aware of the pressures towards 'realism' that operate, with a kind of hidden ubiquity, even in those areas of culture that have left it behind. Fantasy is the key battleground. Presumably you don't think that fantasy is a disreputable and frivolous mode of art, or you wouldn't want to write it. But it's very possible – it's even likely – that you have unknowingly supped enough of the black milk of literary respectability to think that fantasy ought to be judged by the criteria of realism. The way this mostly works in contemporary fantasy literature is a feeling that writers need to make their worlds violent, oppressive and horrible places. It's fair enough to have dragons, prophecy, magic spells and so on – although not too many of them, since they're not 'realistic' – but the societies of this imaginary medieval kingdom must involve humans preying on other humans like wild animals, torture and rape commonplace, a universal cynicism the order of the day.

I'm not registering a squeamishness when I say this. Brutalism can be the motor behind great writing. My problem when people say to themselves, not 'I shall write a fantasy novel in which people – and especially women – are brutalized, tortured and raped because I find aesthetic sadism appealing', but instead 'I shall write a world a bit like Middle Earth but much more violent and horrible, because Middle Earth is a medieval-esque world and the actual Middle Ages was a horrible time'. The cloven hoof of realism flashes out.

If you want to write a historical novel set in medieval Europe showing how horrible life was back then, do so. You'll need to do some in-depth research, and of course you'll need to leave out the dragons and talking swords; but maybe you'll write something powerful. And if you want to write a Grimdark fantasy in which you inflict continual suffering and misery upon your characters – why, do so! Maybe it'll be brilliant. Just don't be under any illusions about what is going on. The geeky young male would-be author who says, 'in my fantasy book warriors ride to battle on the backs of giant were-unicorns and the hero lives in a sky palace built of rainclouds that fire lightning bolts on to his enemies below and also all the women are oppressed and raped *I'm sorry that's just how things were back then*' – this feller is telling us almost nothing about actual medieval life, and an awful lot about his own subconscious resentments and obsessions.

I'm not saying that your fantasy should be unrealistic. On the contrary, if your fantasy world is implausible, readers won't buy it. The point is that 'realism' is not the same thing as realistic. Realism in this specialized literary historical sense is a commitment to the sort of verisimilitude that reproduces all the external phenomena of life as accurately as possible. When Zola wrote his novels he aimed, by detailed research and note-taking and a writing style crammed with a huge amount of closely observed 'actual' detail, to give his readers a sense of what it was actually like living in nineteenth-century Paris. Fantasy works by a different logic – like SF, it sets out to represent the world without reproducing it. It includes things that are not in the real world – magic, ghosts and gods and so on. But these things are not arbitrary inventions; they speak metaphorically to the lived experience. Metaphor, irony, poetry, symbolism and all the currencies of fantasy need to connect with our sense of the way the world actually is, or the result will seem only wafer thin. In the context we are talking about here, to call a fantasy 'realistic' means more than that it is internally consistent and vividly developed: it means that it connects with real aspects of the readers' psychology.

Come at this another way: very broadly, readers of fantasy pick up their favourite books because those books give them something missing from the world as it actually is (and missing, usually, from artistic representations of the way the world actually is, such as 'Realism'). We might call this thing 'enchantment', a sense of magic. A special something the world of the story has that isn't there in our world.

Fantasy carries us away. We want it to: that is why we go to it in the first place. This 'carrying away' need not be mere escapism. It seems to me that the greatest fantasy novels aren't 'escapist' in the bland sense of the word, actually. But the key thing to understand when you set about developing your fantasy world is that the magic depends for its psychological and artistic force not upon what it allows your characters to do, but upon the ways in which it is limited. If Gandalf can simply sweep his wand and magic the One Ring out of existence, there is not only no story but there is nothing whatsoever. In the same way, it is the kryptonite, not the superpowers, that determines how effective a Superman story will be.

For example: let's say your fantasy realm is a place where magic works. That's fine: magic is a way in which certain special people become empowered, and many people who feel themselves disempowered in their actual humdrum lives find consolation and excitement in fantasies of empowerment. But these powers will only work, in a fictional sense, if they are limited; and the more they are limited the more dramatically effective they will be.

It may be that your characters have magic powers, but are faced by adversaries who have the same or even greater magic powers. In the *Harry Potter* novels, it is not just that magic is something hard-won and developed over many years; it is that the evil characters have access to greater powers than the good characters. In other words, there is both a cost and a danger associated with the (exciting, transporting) ability to wave your wand and shout 'expelliarmus!'

It could be that your character has magic powers, but lives in a world where magical ability is hated and persecuted, as in the BBC serial *Merlin*. This has the dramatic usefulness of meaning that you can construct stories in which the magical protagonist cannot simply wave his magic wand and eliminate whatever opposition is powering the dynamic of the story.

Perhaps your character has magical abilities but only of a very limited sort. Gandalf, for instance, can do some magical things, but not very many. Maybe your character has magic powers but the use of those powers costs him or her in some non-trivial way. Maybe (as with the ability to see the future in Stephen King's *The Dead Zone*) using the magic weakens and even slowly kills the user, so that it must be rationed. The most potent realization of this kind of magic is M.D. Lachlan's *Wolfsangel* novels, where Viking witches acquire magical powers only after the most horrible set of ritual deprivations and physical suffering.

More dramatically effective even than this, I think, is if the cost is carried by somebody else. This is a very dramatically powerful idea that begins with Dostoevsky, and reaches a kind of short-story perfection in the Ursula Le Guin short story 'The Ones Who Walk away from Omelas'. Say you have magic powers, and that you genuinely mean to use those powers to right wrongs and make the world a better place for everybody. But say you only assume those powers when somebody else suffers. If a child is tortured according to a particular ritual, you acquire your potency. Remember: in this story, you are using your powers for good – to defeat Sauron, or cure the plague, or bring about utopia. But in order to be able to do these things, somebody else must suffer.

If you revolve this idea in your head, you will need to work out where you think the biting point is. Maybe you feel that power purchased even at the price of *one* other human being's discomfort is morally tainted and should be declined. Maybe you feel it depends on the nature of the harm you do in order to acquire the powers. What if it involves locking a child in a cell for 24 hours without food and water? Would it be worth doing this to acquire magical powers to defeat a larger evil? If you think so, then you're already on the slope and you may find that it has been surprisingly well lubricated. Would it be worth acquiring the powers to defeat Sauron or bring about utopia if the cost was that the child was physically tortured? What if the child had to be killed? It's only one child, and by defeating Sauron you could save tens of thousands of lives! Well, fair enough; does that then mean that you would countenance the murder of a dozen children to get your powers? That's still a drop in the bucket compared to the thousands of lives you would save! Soon enough you're in a position where six dozen children are being tortured to death in order to give you the power to fight your enemy. That's all right! You're the good guy, right?

Write flash fiction

You know how much you can type in one hour: set that as your word limit (and if you don't know, then you'll find out if you do this exercise!).

You are going to write a short story based on the idea in the two paragraphs above. This kind of scratch writing, done quickly and as roughly as needs be over a limited time frame, is called 'flash fiction'. This is what you do.

First, work out your initial set-up: two characters, or more if you're feeling ambitious; a world in which magic works, but with some major cost attached to it in terms of the suffering of others. Take as long as you need over this (don't go crazy – not days and days); the clock doesn't start until you actually start writing. One tip: don't be over-ambitious. You're going to have to write the whole story in just an hour. Aim for a brief set-up, established (for instance) in the dialogue between your two deuteragonists, then a quick development in which there is a 'turn', or a new perspective on the situation.

Now set your timer, remove all other distractions, and write your story for one hour.

Stop! Set it aside. We're going to come back to it later.

Tolkien and anti-Tolkien

John Ronald Reuel Tolkien

J.R.R. Tolkien (1892–1973) was first a soldier, and afterwards an English academic, writer and philologist of great distinction. He is, of course, most famous for his high-fantasy novels *The Hobbit* (1937), *The Lord of the Rings* (1954–5) and *The Silmarillion* (1977), three works that utilize different styles (the children's tale, the heroic narrative and a more concise annals mode respectively) to tell stories set in Tolkien's imaginary world of Middle Earth. This world, variously Dark Age, medieval and later in quasi-historical style, populated by different 'races' of humans, elves, dwarfs, hobbits and orcs, and interpenetrated with magic, proved prodigiously influential on fantasy being written in the second half of the twentieth century.

J.R.R. Tolkien is the inescapable name where the resurgence of fantasy is concerned. He enjoyed a small success with his great children's book *The Hobbit*, but it wasn't until the triple-decker *The Lord of the Rings* became a paperback bestseller in the USA that he became culturally significant. Sales continued to rise; thousands upon thousands of imitators wrote second-world fantasy novels patently influenced by Tolkien; and then Peter Jackson's globally blockbusting movies, first of *The Lord of the Rings* and then of *The Hobbit*, cemented his success. Now it wouldn't be wrong to say that the style of fantasy Tolkien wrote has become the dominant mode;

many people, when they think of 'Heroic fantasy', think, essentially, of Tolkien and the following elements:

- A coherently realized secondary world, based on pre-Industrial-Revolution Europe
- A world divided between different 'races'; both 'good' (immortal elves, stocky dwarves, mortal men and a race of 'little people' who become proxy figures for the reader) and 'evil' (orcs, goblins, trolls, balrogs and the like)
- A society in which magical powers are real, and in which magical animals, like dragons, werewolves and giant spiders, actually exist
- A world with a detailed backstory 'history' that reaches back thousands of years in time
- A present determined by a world-spanning battle between 'good' and 'evil'
- A main story that follows the rise from obscurity of some unregarded 'little person' (a hobbit, a goatherd, a potboy, a pig scratcher's daughter) to a position of global importance, by means of a quest, or equivalent, that tests his or her fortitude, bravery and luck.

These are clichés, of course, and – like all clichés – are where you should start from (with a view to upending and remixing them) rather than where you should end up. Why make your fantasy realm a version of Europe? What's wrong with pre-Industrial Asia, Africa or South America? Should 'good' and 'evil' be so cut-and-dried and unambiguously determined? Is it like that in the real world?

As I say, a great many novels have been published in this 'Tolkienian' tradition; and it continues to be influential. Many writers are inspired to write either by Tolkien himself or by writers directly influenced by Tolkien. Examples include:

- Terry Brooks's *Shannara* novels
- Stephen Donaldson's stories of 'The Land'
- Raymond Feist's *Midkemia* stories
- Ursula Le Guin's peerless *Earthsea* stories
- Robert Jordan's interminable *Wheel of Time* novels
- Patrick Rothfuss's *The Name of the Wind* and its sequels.

Popular games in this tradition include Dungeons and Dragons and, to come a little more up to date, World of Warcraft.

If this is what you want to do, then I commend you. You may like to use the nom de plume 'Dan Jenson-Dragons'.

It may take a moment for that gag to sink in.

As influential as Tolkien has been, a tradition defined almost wholly in opposition to what Tolkien was doing has been almost as influential. Michael Moorcock, the author of more fantasy novels than can be counted on the fingers of a dozen people, has always hated the 'Tolkien' school of fantasy writing: it is, he argues in his study of the genre *Wizardry and Wild Romance*, a fundamentally cosy and bourgeois form of art, shaped by the broadly sexist and racist attitudes of the English upper-middle classes. 'Epic Pooh', he calls it. In its place, Moorcock invokes a rather different tradition, reaching back to William Hope Hodgson, William Morris and Mervyn Peake. On the American side of the Atlantic, where the Dickensian castle-gothic of Peake's *Gormenghast* (1946–59) books are less well known, there is a more violent 'barbarian' tradition of fantasy – sometimes called 'sword and sorcery', to distinguish it from Tolkienian 'heroic fantasy' – out of Robert Howard's *Conan* stories, via Edgar Rice Burroughs's *Tarzan* tales and Fritz Leiber's wittily cynical writing. This in turn leads through to modern 'Grimdark' writing, where nobody is honourable and Might is Right. George R.R. Martin's ongoing fantasy sequence *A Song of Fire and Ice* is surely the most successful and popular Grimdark fantasy. It owes a lot to Tolkien, I think, but is determined as much by its reaction to the more 'idealized' aspects of Tolkien's world.

Key idea

'Grimdark' has become the standard way of referring to fantasies that turn their backs on the more uplifting, Pre-Raphaelite visions of idealized medievaliana, and instead stress how nasty, brutish, short and, er, dark life back then 'really' was. I put 'really' in inverted commas there, since Grimdark usually has very little to do with actual historical re-imagining and everything to do with a sense that our present world is a cynical, disillusioned ultraviolent place. The word was coined from the tagline to the *Warhammer 40,000* series of novels and games: 'In the grim darkness of the far future there is only war.'

If you're going to write this kind of fantasy, my advice would be: leaven the grimness with humour. Joe Abercrombie is a good example of somebody who knows how to do this (if, indeed, 'Abercrombie' actually exists: there are rumours that he is an actor paid to front the committee-composed productions of a mysterious cabal). His *First Law* series, starting with *The Blade Itself* (2006), is immersive and readable, and its violence and refusal of idealism is always wittily and engagingly handled.

 Key idea

'Grimdark' fantasy should not be confused with 'Poldark' fantasy. The latter is about a mythically reimagined Cornwall. The former is about axes cleaving people's skulls, rendered in repulsive and minute detail.

What is strong in the 'anti-Tolkien' tradition is a refusal to collaborate with racism, sexism or other modes of prejudice (conscious or otherwise) in one's worldbuilding. Women's roles were more limited in medieval Europe than is, broadly speaking, the case today; but you are writing for today, not for a medieval audience.

If you want to avoid the charge of sexism (I suppose it's possible you don't want to avoid this charge. Possible but not acceptable), it is not enough to include a token 'kick-ass' female assassin character; especially if said character wears a tight-fighting leather costume and sports a DD-cup bosom. You need to think through the pervasiveness of sexism more than that.

The representation of women as 'fantasies' rather than actual beings is one of the oldest, most pervasive and most pernicious aspects of human culture. This has largely been powered by a heterosexual male impulse towards an erotic simplification of the female, rendered purely in instrumental terms (for masturbatory transport, for instance). It is beyond the scope of this study to deal with 'pornography' in the largest sense, although pornography of course is a fantasy literature – although one of a rather limited sort.

Similarly, if you aim to steer clear of accusations of racism, it's probably a good idea not to make all your evil characters dark skinned and all your immortal elven heroes and heroines hyperbolically Aryan and fair (although that is what Tolkien did). And if your imagined world is one in which the orcs are all black and the heroes all blonde and pale, it's not a sufficient redress to make one of the heroic band of questers brown-skinned.

Some general thoughts on worldbuilding

The built world is there to facilitate the story, not the other way around – your readers will come to you in the first instance for a gripping story, and get drawn into the immersive experience of a well-built world only secondarily. But that doesn't mean you can afford to be sloppy about your worldbuilding. An inconsistent, sketchy, illogically built world will bounce the reader out of your story.

You don't need to spend months specifying every single minor detail, but you do need to put in enough time and thought to get some basic things clear in your head. Your world will involve many people. What do they eat? Where do they get their food? How are they supplied with clean water? Who tends to their injuries? What happens if their houses catch fire? What happens to their bodily wastes? What features in your world tend to people's spiritual needs, their needs for entertainment and exercise? Actual societies in our world run according to particular scarcity-based economies: is this true of your world? How do they allocate their resources? What do they use for money? Do they make their own clothes and furniture? Is there a peasant class – and if so, why do they put up with being actually or effectively enslaved?

Jo Walton

'If someone called John Smith is normal now, it won't necessarily always be normal. There's a thing I call STP from the chemistry expression for "standard temperature and pressure" meaning the unexamined assumed norms – and for SF you want to consider whether you want today's social STP or not.'

Consistency is particularly important when it comes to integrating whatever novum or point of difference it is that makes your story fantasy or SF. It's fine to use historical research to give a sense of plausibility to fantasy worldbuilding, but beware of two things. One is that a version of medieval Europe that includes things like 'functioning magic', or 'actual flying dragons, and an air force of knights mounted on the saddled backs of giant eagles' is not going to be exactly like medieval Europe except for those two things. Those two things would completely change the entire dynamic of the built world, and you need to think of the many ways in which the repercussions work themselves out. Two relates to questions of diversity. Medieval Europe was a pretty horrible place to be a woman or in a racial minority. When you write your fantasy, of course, you don't want simply to reproduce that sexism and racism. But neither can you simply reproduce all the structures of power but with equal numbers of women and people of colour in positions of authority. That authority was constructed around logics of loyalty and fear that actualized stifling in-group identity and fear of the other. A multicultural society is a great good; but the reason why medieval Europe wasn't such a society isn't that 'it just happened not to be'.

Steampunk has a similar problem. The reason why 'difference engine' computers, steam-powered zeppelin travelling across the Atlantic and Captain Nemo's *Nautilus* weren't features of the actual nineteenth century is not that they happened not to be invented. These things (I mean computers, commercial airliners and nuclear submarines) are the epiphenomena of complicated and deep-rooted social and economic realities.

To speculate on the widespread adoption of a new piece of technology into a whole society is to imagine the ways in which the whole society is reshaped.

 Consistency

Emerson famously said, 'A foolish consistency is the hobgoblin of little minds.' He had a point. Fortunately, in science fiction and fantasy we actively welcome curious and foolish creatures like hobgoblins, and strive to make a proper home for them.

A major aspect of consistency is the way the various technologies (or magics) you have made up would interact with one another. Here is a slightly facile example:

The *Star Trek* universe is supplied with, among many other technological advances, two particularly prominent novums: 'phasers' and 'teleportation'. But why have the former if we have the latter? Wouldn't it make more sense not to fire line-of-sight phasers, but rather to teleport bullets and explosives directly into the bodies of our enemies? (Phasers have 'stun' settings; but there's nothing stopping us teleporting sleeping drugs or other incapacitants into our enemies' bodies if we wanted to.) We could take this further: given the advantages of teleportation, wouldn't it make sense to concentrate research on that, rather than develop expensive, cumbersome starships? Better to teleport directly to another planet than spend months flying there. (You might be tempted to address this problem by simply imposing a restriction on teleportation by authorial fiat – 'it only works over relatively short distances' – and that's fine; but you do need to make sure such fiats do not strike the reader as arbitrary, or as merely tweaking the rules of your worldbuilding to enable your plot. Besides, in *Star Trek into Darkness* (2013) we discover that it is possible to teleport from Earth to Planet Klingon![1]

I don't say this merely to nit-pick. These are not 'problems' in the worldbuilding of *Star Trek* so much as they are opportunities in the worldbuilding of *your* forthcoming SF masterpiece.

What does all this mean for how you should write?

Both science fiction and fantasy are metaphorical literatures, because they seek to represent the world without reproducing it. Don't be afraid of metaphor; it is centrally what we do.

---

1 We also discover that death can be cured, and Bones now knows how. This will surely result in a world where the pressures of immortality become the main motor for subsequent stories – unless Bones himself turns evil, and tries to leverage his knowledge into ultimate power. One other thing that has always bothered me about the *Star Trek* universe – wouldn't the Holodeck completely replace the concept of a 'built environment'? At the very least, there should no longer be such a thing as 'furniture' on any starship.

Science fiction and fantasy are non-Realist in conception. They may be Realist in form – that is to say, you may (as many SF writers have) develop your fantastic premise with scrupulous attention to verisimilitude. But the central premise of your story will be something that isn't in the real world. This is the central feature of both genres, and something about which you should be absolutely unembarrassed. Revel in your novum. Celebrate it. And take on board the moral of it. Make new! Whenever you are faced with something old and stale and conventionalized, think of a way to unsettle and rewire that oldness.

Science fiction, whether you consider it an ancient, nineteenth-century or a modern phenomenon, has always been a literature centrally about how we cope with newness entering into the world. This makes it profound as well as cool.

Fantasy is also about newness, although not quite in the same way. The deal with fantasy is freshness, about finding a way of adding a lustre and magic to what is otherwise a dull and mundane sense of the world.

This means that, among many other things, you need to treat this book, the very one you are reading now, with a proper sense of wariness. If I tell you that something is an essential rule of writing, handed down through the ages and hallowed by time – think how you can subvert it. The most I would say in my own defence is that you need to understand the rules in order to be able to subvert the rules. But as long as it works, it is good.

Science fiction and fantasy are the great literatures of imaginative possibility. This is why they offer such spectacular potential to a writer.

Summary

This chapter has aimed to sketch out a sense of what science fiction and fantasy are: a thumbnail sense of the history of the genre and the main subdivisions – 'hard' science fiction versus 'soft', fantasy in the heroic Tolkienian tradition versus some of the alternatives that have been developed. Connected to this is a brief discussion of the broader approaches of 'worldbuilding', with a stress upon how you should work towards a 'consistency' of imagined universes – not out of a small-minded love for consistency as such, but because moments of inconsistency can always be levered into new writing possibilities.

Workshop

I'm going to introduce a larger-scale writing project at this stage – the composition of a whole (short) novel, science fiction or fantasy. At the very least I want you to conceive, plot out and write the key scenes of this novel; but if you're feeling especially energized it ought to be possible to draft the whole thing over about a month. There is a popular discipline in science fiction/fantasy called #NaNoMoWri, when people commit to devoting the month of November to writing a complete novel. There's no reason why you should wait until November to do this!

Nothing is better practice for writing novels than writing whole novels. If the work you produce is good, you might even see it into print; but even if it's no good you learn more by doing than you ever can by theorizing and planning.

It is, I know, a big ask. So we're going to break it down. The first step is: work out what the core idea of your novel is going to be. This will be either (a) an idea you already have, and are itching to develop, or (b) an idea you generate for this task.

Where to next?

If you're going with the second option, then the next chapter is all about how to have cool ideas for SF and fantasy stories and novels.

3

How to have original ideas

Writers of 'regular' novels get their ideas from various sources. Commonly they mine their own life experiences – although the problem here is that, unless you've led an unusually varied or interesting life, you'll mine this seam dry within a couple of novels. Certainly, 'real life' is a good source for ideas, because such ideas come pre-supplied with plausibility and vitality (since they must at least be plausible enough to have actually happened). Writers of science fiction and fantasy are well advised to bear this in mind. Our stock-in-trade is stuff that has never happened (or never happened yet) in anyone's life. This means that we need to pay closer attention than other writers to keeping it 'real'.

Many writers make a point of reading several newspapers with their notebooks open beside them. Contemporary newspapers are fine for this, especially the smaller-scale and less noticed stories. Even better are old newspapers – there's a wealth of these online, and browsing them turns up all sorts of fascinating forgotten nuggets of story and characters-in-action. Other writers keep dream diaries, or else rely on ideas simply popping into their heads.

These strategies have their uses for writers of science fiction and fantasy, too; but they take us only so far. The bald fact is that most readers come to our genres for more elevated story ideas, more striking novelty and out-of-this-world-ness in their premises. The big idea. The high concept. And this chapter will tell you how to generate such ideas.

Can they be synthesized so easily? you ask. Aren't they like lightning strikes, scorching the writer's brain from a clear blue sky?

Well, yes they can. And yes, sometimes they are like lightning strikes – if such ideas swoop, aquiline, into your heads, then bravo! I shake your hand, and steer you by your elbow into this charming little side-street café to buy you a congratulatory drink. But such thunderbolts are by definition rare, and even rarer is the writer who can subsist, imaginatively, upon them. To anticipate the 'How to live by your writing' chapter from later in the book, if you are serious about being a writer then you'll need to be ready to write more than just the occasional story. You need to say 'yes' to every paying commission (at least, every paying commission that isn't offering insultingly low pay rates). If somebody is ready to pay you a healthy chunk of money to write a story for an anthology of 'original Napoleonic War zombie fiction', submission deadline two weeks from now, it's not enough to settle yourself in a lawn chair in your back garden and wait, expectantly, for the giant neon fishbone of electricity to come lancing down out of the sky. You need to get straight to work.

So this chapter will give you some ideas on how to have, shape and develop ideas. Ideas about ideas sounds a little meta, I know; and actually 'meta-ideas' as a useful tool in the imaginative artist's arsenal. But rest assured: it is not hard.

Indeed, it's so easy that I positively scatter this chapter with original story ideas. I count 38 different premises for interesting stories – all of which you are free to pick up and run with, if you choose. My point is not the story ideas themselves: it is the process by which those story ideas are generated.

Focus point

Good ideas can come into your head at any time of the day or night. Accordingly, you should carry a notebook or other note-taking format with you at all times. Ideas are like peas; they need to be frozen as soon as picked. This is especially true at sleepy-time. Because of the way the mind is structured, falling asleep involves a relaxing of the borderline between waking and dreaming states, and for that reason this interlude is remarkably productive of original ideas. If you are lying in your bed, lights out, drifting off, and a good idea for a story or novel pops into your head, do not say to yourself, 'Cool! I'll jot that down in the morning' and continue drifting off. On no account just go to sleep. Instead, turn on the light, ignore the complaints from your partner, scrabble around for a pen and paper and jot the idea down then and there. If you don't, I promise you: you will not remember it in the morning. Oh, you'll remember that you had a really cool idea just before you went to sleep – you just won't recall what the idea was. And my bitter personal experience assures you that nothing more irritating can be conceived. Heed me on this: as soon as the great idea arrives, write it down.

There's one thing to keep in mind as you read this chapter – and, indeed, as you read the whole of this book. An idea can be a number of things: a premise, a cool concept, a wrinkle in the laws of physics, an aspect of magic previously unconsidered, a story twist. It can even be an image or a phrase. Lewis Carroll found the line 'for the Snark *was* a Boojum, you see' in his head and couldn't seem to get rid of it, despite not knowing what either a Snark or a Boojum might be. He was compelled, eventually, to write his great poem *The Hunting of the Snark* just to make sense of it (the phrase became the last line of the poem). John Fowles found himself haunted by the image of a beautiful woman in a cloak standing on the stone pier at Lyme Regis, on the southern English coast, looking mournfully out to sea. Because the image wouldn't let him go, he constructed a story to explain it, and then wrote this out as his novel *The French Lieutenant's Woman*. To step down from the sublime to the ridiculous, I myself once woke up from a dream in which the planet Jupiter loomed impossibly vast in the Earthly sky – I took the image, worked out a possible explanation for it, and wrote the whole thing up as a short novel, for which the nicely dactylic title *Jupiter Magnified* suggested itself.

An image or an idea might stick in your head, but for it to be of use it must have dramatic potential. What this means is that you must get into the habit of taking any idea you have, any striking image or notion, and asking yourself: where is the drama, here?

What I mean by drama is conflict. If there's no conflict, there's no story.

This is one of the few observations I can make about story-making that is universally true; but it is particularly true of science fiction and fantasy. This is because science fiction and fantasy are more likely than other kinds of fiction to trade in compensatory fantasies of empowerment. And the problem with such fantasies, however much temporary psychological satisfaction they give you, is that they dissolve away the dramatic potential of good storytelling, as salt does a slug. Superman is a cool idea but, without kryptonite to disempower him, all we have is a smoothly empty paean to power as such.

In real life you often feel put-upon or ignored; your nine-to-five in a mid-size office supply company is a drag. But in 'the magic world of story' you are a queen with the power to command dragons, and incredibly hunky men crowd around you to do your bidding. Or you are a teenager who has to haul their complaining bones out of bed every weekday morning and trudge off to the most boring school in western civilization – but in 'the magic world of story' you go to Pigblemish School of Magic and Wonderfulness, and your life is one of spellbinding charm and glamour. Or you are a nine-stone weakling – except in story, where you are Thor, god of Thunder and Massive Biceps and a *Really* Cool Hairdo. Or your life is confined to the suburban run between dropping the kids at school, going to work and returning to your tiny house; and therefore in your imagination you span the galaxy in a sleek and hideously-beweaponed starship powered by engines of ultimate thrust.

I'm not trying to be dismissive when I say all this – really, I'm not. I take seriously the grinding effect that disempowerment – real or perceived – has upon people; and the imaginative escape of great stories is a great instrument of psychological and moral good. I'm not mocking. I'm doing something different. I'm asking you to look at the empowering story idea from the point of view of the writer instead of the reader.

What I'm trying to do here is introduce to you one idea: it is not power that makes a great story, but the obstacles to power. It is not achievement that makes a good story, but the obstacles to achievement. Falling in love with an adoringly beautiful individual and living happily ever after is not a drama; *Romeo and Juliet* is a drama. It is the kryptonite, not the godlike powers of Superman, that makes the story.

Nabokov, on the idea that gave birth to his novel *Lolita*

'The initial shiver of inspiration was somehow prompted by a newspaper story about an ape in the Jardin des Plantes who, after months of coaxing by a scientist, produced the first drawing ever charcoaled by an animal: this sketch showed the bars of the poor creature's cage.'

The problem with stories of compensatory empowerment is that they dissolve away the dramatic tension necessary for great stories.

It must become second nature in you to challenge all the beguiling fantasies of achievement that occur to you, to think in terms of obstacles. This in turn is going to work out one way or another:

- either the obstacles are, ultimately, overcome, as in *The Lord of the Rings* (and here it is the fact that we care about the characters, and therefore feel the cost paid by the characters in achieving their goals, that is vital)
- or the obstacles are not overcome, as in *Romeo and Juliet* (in which case the tragic effect is created by the thought of what might have been).

Focus point

Identify your obstacles carefully: the more nuanced and real-life the better. Here's one word, offered as an encapsulation of much that is wrong in the writing of science fiction and fantasy: *supervillain*.

Now, supervillains can be great: hissable pantomime baddies can be very memorable. But they are – always – limiting, dramatically speaking. If you are writing a story with a supervillain in it, then you are writing melodrama. I have no problem with melodrama, as it happens; but you need to be able to do more as a writer than just the broad stroke, good-versus-evil caricature stuff. There are two problems with supervillains:

- They do not occur in real life. Real people can do evil things, and many do; but nobody simply is evil. Actual people are always rounded and complicated. Even Hitler was kind to his pet dog. Writing characters of ultimate evil into your story will coarsen and cartoonify your work.

- They are a lazy strategy, writerly-wise. If the best you can think of by way of putting story obstacles in the path of your otherwise too effortlessly achieving Thor is to chuck a cackling Loki in his path, then you're not trying hard enough. If your lovingly detailed and painstakingly mapped-out fantasy realm feels dramatically inert, then introducing a character called Lord Vile and giving him a horde of shambling horrors is a clumsy way of zizzing up your potential story.

The problem may be the impulse to externalize the obstacles your story needs. You've come up with a new kind of superhero, handsome, likeable and virtuous. What problems will he face? Professor Malignity and his Giant Vermicious Robots of Doom are more than just a cliché: they are a dull cliché. Why should we care about the professor? How can so second-hand a notion feel like anything other than going through the motions?

If the drama in your story connects, symbolically or directly, with the sorts of dramas that shape real people's lives, then your story will gain in power and impact. Real people do not have to overcome evil galactic professors who have spent seven years on Pluto building worm-like robots to conquer the Earth and so return that planetoid to its former status as fully fledged planet. Real people come with problems like weariness, boredom, anxiety and the quotidian struggles of making ends meet. I'm not saying that your stories have to reproduce such problems literally. On the contrary, the strength of science fiction and fantasy is its ability to embody eloquent symbolic apprehensions of reality. But you are not stupid: you know when those symbols have lost the quality of lived experience.

Action in character is better than characters in action. 'Characters in action' is fine, of course; but we need to care about them.

There is one last thing to say about the whole 'goodies versus baddies' story premise or, more specifically, about its limitations. Your story sets up some likeable heroes and heroines, characters with which we can identity and for whom we will root. Then it presents us with some antagonist who is simply evil and nothing more – Lord Vile of Obsidian Magical Foulness, Insectoid Alien invaders from the Planet Cockroachia. Given this set-up, the story can only be about the *practical* challenges of overcoming adversity. It'll be about the hows, not the whys; and the preferred outcome will never be in doubt. Right and wrong have been too crisply delineated. In fact, an antagonist need not be wholly and irremediably evil to work as an antagonist. In fact, the less irremediably evil your antagonist is, the better she or he will work.

Why does your antagonist want what s/he wants? What are his/her motivations? Does she have a point?

A word of warning here: a desperately common strategy for 'explaining' the malignancy of villainous characters is to reveal that they were abused as children. Why is Hannibal Lecter so psychotic? Childhood abuse! What is the motivation for the many crimes perpetrated by Angus Thermopyle (the main character in Stephen Donaldson's *Gap* series of SF novels)? Childhood abuse! Why is Voldemort so evil? Because the other kids at the orphanage were so beastly to him!

I urge and exhort you to steer clear of this tiresome narrative strategy. It tends to trivialize actual childhood abuse (a ghastly and very present problem) in a way that borders on sheer impertinence.

Prototype story – *Antigone*

This Greek myth, and more especially the play of that name written by the Athenian dramatist Sophocles in the fifth century BCE, has been acclaimed by many as embodying the quintessential tragic dilemma. The story is this: seven Theban warriors have betrayed their city and attempted to conquer it. They have been defeated and killed, and Sophocles' play is concerned with the aftermath of their attempt. The Theban king Creon has decreed that the traitors be denied the burial rites that ancient Greeks considered essential – their corpses must be left outside the city as carrion. Cleon decrees that this is not because he is wicked or vindictive, but for the good of the city as a whole. His son, Haemon, is in love with the beautiful Antigone; but Antigone's brother Polynices was one of the seven traitors. She knows Creon's decree and she is loyal to her city; but she loved her brother and cannot bear the thought that his body is going to be denied proper burial rites.

This is the set-up for Sophocles' play. It is not that Creon is a wicked tyrant. *He* is doing what he thinks best for the collective good of the whole city. Nor is it that Antigone is a habitual law-breaker or delinquent; she is also doing what she considers to be her unshirkable duty. What makes Sophocles' play so powerful is that both these conceptions of doing the right thing have merit but they are nonetheless incompatible with each other. Creon and Antigone must both act; and both of them have (as they see it) right on their side; but their actions will bring them into implacable conflict with each other. The result is a 'conflict' powering a story of enduring heft and richness. It is a story that engages you intellectually – what do you think takes precedence, the rights of one individual or the rights of the people as a whole? – *because* it engages you emotionally.

If you retold this story with Creon as a Hitler-style tyrant and Antigone a purely virtuouous heroine; or with Creon as a brave leader struggling to hold his people together and Antigone as a spoiled brat who puts her own selfish desires ahead of everyone else's need – in either case the story as a whole would lose force.

After all, almost all survivors of childhood abuse do not grow up to become supervillains. It's also a lazy story gimmick, the sign of a writer prepared to gesture in only the vaguest sense at the truth that character is complex and motivation a folded and pleated thing.

So: story ideas in science fiction and fantasy should be neat; but the neat-y isn't sufficient without the gritty.

Let's get down to that nitty gritty. How does one invent cool story ideas?

Ursula Le Guin

'I have never found anywhere, in the domain of art, that you don't have to walk to. (There is quite an array of jets, buses and hacks which you can ride to Success; but that is a different destination.) It is a pretty wild country. There are, of course, roads. Great artists make the roads; good teachers and good companions can point them out. But there ain't no free rides, baby. No hitchhiking. And if you want to strike out in any new direction – you go alone. With a machete in your hand and the fear of God in your heart.'

Inventing story ideas (I): clearing the decks

One difficulty in science fiction (and, to a lesser extent, fantasy) is the backlist. Hundreds of thousands of novels and short stories have been published in the genre before you even pick up a pen or turn on your laptop – every one of them embodying a story idea original enough in its time to merit payment and publication. This is a brute fact that makes it hard to have an original idea, and it can lead you into a cul-de-sac of 'there's nothing new under the sun' despair. I was at a one-day literary convention in London once with another writer, who shall of course remain nameless. This other writer was famous for his 'mainstream' novels, and over coffee he said, 'I'm glad to meet you, Adam, because actually I've been thinking of writing a science-fiction story.' 'Oh yes?' I replied, my heart leaping up. 'Yes,' he said. 'I was reading in the *New Scientist* that the distances between the stars are so enormous that any spaceship travelling from Earth to the stars could take hundreds of years – so that entire generations of crew would be born, grow up, grow old and die, to be replaced by other generations and so on. As soon as I read that, I thought to myself: what a wonderful premise for a story!' I waited for a moment for him to say a little more, but he didn't do anything other than smile at me and look pleased with himself. 'Well, indeed!' I said, a little tentatively. 'It *is* a great set-up for a story, I quite agree. Of course, a few – quite a few, if I'm honest – so-called Generation Starship stories have already been published in science fiction. You might want to read Robert Heinlein's *Orphans of the Sky*, or Brian Aldiss's *Non-Stop*, or Steven Baxter's ...' He held up his meaty hand like a traffic policeman. 'No, no,' he told me, airily. 'I don't want to get bogged down with all that. It will only sap my creative energy.' And so he went on to write his story, and effectively to reinvent the wheel of the Generation Starship yarn. The result was a stale, second-hand and in the end forgettable book.

But his desire not to step into the *Wreck-It-Ralph*-y chocolate flavoured Nesquik-sand of the backlist was perfectly understandable. I've been reading science fiction and fantasy all my life, and plan to continue doing so until I die, but I've barely scratched the surface of all the stuff that's been produced. It will help if you are already a fan, not because that means you'll know everything, but you will at least know the most celebrated examples. If a friend came to you and said, 'I've got a great idea for a novel! It's about a school for witches and wizards!' and you said, 'Oh, like *Harry Potter*?' and they looked quizzically at you and said, 'Harry What-er?' you'd want to suggest they at least glance at J.K. Rowling's books before proceeding.

So if you have an idea, don't plunge straight in. Clear the decks first. It won't take you long. Spend ten minutes googling the premise. If you've had (say) a great idea for a time travel story, then go to the online *Encyclopedia of Science Fiction* at www.sf-encyclopedia.com/ (edited by Clute, Nicholls and Langford) and read through the entry on 'Time travel'. Use Wikipedia. Talk to those of your friends you can trust not to steal your brilliant ideas. When Paul McCartney wrote 'Yesterday', he was convinced he had plagiarised the tune from some other song, so familiar did it sound in his own ears. It was only after he played it to the other Beatles and they told him they didn't recognize it from anywhere else that he went ahead with it.

Moreover, this process can be turned around so as to make it a positive good. Researching an old idea can spark off original versions of that idea that you can use as a writer. Reading the *Harry Potter* novels and thinking, 'Wouldn't it be great to write a story about a magical school' is a perfectly noble thing, provided only that you resolve not to plagiarize or copy. Instead, think about the way Rowling developed her basic idea and, more to the point, think about the ways it could have been done differently.

For example, the world of *Harry Potter* concentrates on a magical school, and also includes magical versions of a number of 'real world' institutions, among them magical government ministries, magical prisons, magical sports teams and so on. What institutions are not present in the novels? How might a magical hospital, say, work? (Clearly, it would have to entail more than simply doctor-witches and surgeon-wizards waving their wands and making all the patients well again; there would have to be more conflict in the idea – the hospital would be for those who could not simply be cured.) What about a magical theatre? A magical NASA? A magical advertising agency? ('*Mag Men*, starring Wizard John Draper'?) How would a magical Mafia differ from the actual Mafia? What might a magical old people's home look like? What happens to a witch or a wizard if they begin suffering from Alzheimer's?

Think of other aspects of the world of magic that could be moved about, and work through the story implications of those adjustments to the rules. For example, what if only children were capable of magic, and the power faded through adolescence to disappear entirely in adulthood? How would a school work if the adult teachers had only the memories of magic, and not the actual powers? How would they maintain discipline? Would it devolve into a *Lord of the Flies*-style scenario? ('Lord of the Flying Broomsticks'.) Would children be put to work in the magical equivalent of sweatshops and factories, generating the magical effect the whole of society needed? How would the non-magical adults achieve and oversee such a thing? Would they feel qualms at exploiting the children, or would they (having been through the experience themselves) simply take it as part of the way the world worked? With any story that involves sharply differentiated good and bad characters, it is always worth asking yourself: how would I rewrite this tale from the point of view of the bad guys? What would *Harry Potter* look like if Malfoy were the central character and we were encouraged to like and identify with him? Would you be able to write a sympathetic version of Voldemort? Let's imagine, for instance, a story about a talented wizard who thought he was trying to bequeath the world a great collective good by overcoming death itself; but who was opposed at every turn by small-minded stick-in-the-muds crying 'Tradition!' and 'Down with innovation!' and so on.

 ## Snapshot exercise

There are lots of questions in the previous two paragraphs: there's a story idea behind the way you, individually, would answer each and every one.

Workshop

Oh, My GIANT Blue Head!

The movie *Megamind* tried the experiment of positioning a 'superhero' film from the point of view of the 'bad guy'. And it's a pretty good movie, although it cheats a little by making Megamind himself basically a nice guy, shuffling its 'superhero' equivalent offstage early on and then bringing on a much worse supervillain for Megamind to fight. (By, in other words, just shifting the standard superhero story template one notch along and thereby leaving it pretty much unchanged.)

Your challenge is to try to rewire a popular heroes-and-villains story so that the 'villain' is positioned at the story's heart.

- What if the elves, men and hobbits of Middle Earth were all white supremacist eugenicists, and Sauron a freedom-fighting leader trying to lead his dark-skinned peoples out of the 'prison' of hellish Mordor, to enjoy equal rights in the country as a whole? Could the novel be rewritten so as to position Sauron as the hero?

- Does Mr Smith in *The Matrix* have a point? What if human beings really are 'a disease of this world, a plague', and your job was to oppose them? Could you rewrite the story of *The Matrix* as if the whole system were a body, the 'agents' antibodies and characters like Neo and Morpheus viruses and cancers?
- William Blake once called Milton 'a true poet, and of the devil's party without knowing it'. He meant that those scenes in Paradise Lost with Satan in them are much more vibrant and alive than the scenes with God talking piously to Jesus. But how would you reconfigure the story Milton tells in his great epic to make the devil into Frodo Baggins, or Neo? Satan, after all, is massively outgunned by God and underdog stories are always popular.

If nothing else, this is a useful exercise for testing the ease with which your villain is defeated in the end. Looking at things from the baddie's point of view will tend to flag up implausibilities, easily countered offences and coincidences.

I'm sure I don't need to say I'm not suggesting that you infringe any published writer's copyright. If you reconfigure the story of *Harry Potter*, you will need to change all the names and specific referents. Copyright law means that while an idea (for instance, the idea of a school for wizards) cannot be copyright protected, the specific iteration of that idea can (that is, the names 'Harry Potter' and 'Hogwarts' and anything directly pertaining to Rowling's imaginative vision). One rule of thumb: if an unwary punter were to buy your 'school for wizards' book thinking it was by J.K. Rowling, she would have a good claim against you in a court of law, and will sue.

So I'm not proposing plagiary. I'm suggesting that researching what has already been written in and around your story idea can be a launchpad to new ideas. I'm going to wind up this section with some particular ideas that occurred to me after reading three of the foundational texts of modern science fiction and fantasy.

1   C.S. Lewis's *The Lion, the Witch and the Wardrobe* is a great children's fantasy story, and one I read over and over as a youngling. Four ordinary children pass through a magic

wardrobe into the fantasy realm of Narnia, a place populated with talking animals and under the malign spell of the White Witch. The children meet Aslan, a lion; defeat the witch; are crowned kings and queens of Narnia, and grow to adulthood in this wonderful place. At the end of the book they are out hunting in the forest when they find themselves back at the wardrobe-portal, and come back through into our world. Here they find themselves children again – for although decades have passed inside Narnia, time in our world has only advanced a few minutes. Now, this is a cool idea – one of many in Lewis's story. But Lewis makes nothing of it. I find myself wondering if this isn't the moment when the story starts getting really interesting. What would it be like to grow to adulthood and then abruptly find yourself returned to a child again, with all the memories and adult apprehensions intact in your mind? What would you do? Would you try to tell adults of your experiences? Would they believe you? Would you be compelled to keep it secret? Would it drive you mad, to be an adult trapped again in the body of a child, with all the restrictions society places on children? Would you use your intellectual maturity to trick people? What about sex – would returning to a prepubescent body be, in effect, a mode of chemical castration? How would your adult knowledge of sexual matters affect the kind of child you then were? All these questions seem to me powerful and interesting ones, in a way more powerful and interesting (because they relate to action in character rather than characters in action) than the ones Lewis actually bases his story on.

2 When I was a young writer, I found myself thinking about the world of **Tolkien's** *Lord of the Rings* – a novel I'd read over and over as a child. Tolkien's Middle Earth is a world pitched somewhere around the late Anglo-Saxon and medieval period of European history, with a few anomalies (the hobbits, with their pipes, waistcoats, kettles and comfortable detached dwelling houses are more like eighteenth-century gentry than medieval warriors). But if *The Lord of the Rings* told the story of a basically medieval world, then what might that world have developed into? What if we fast-forwarded the historical clock to the Middle Earth equivalent of the twentieth century? So I wrote a 40,000 word novella set in such a time and called it

Rings. It concerned a university historian who specialized in the 'medieval' era of his world, and told a story of his unhappy marriage and infidelity. The model, stylistically, was the great US novelists of mid-life crisis twentieth-century fiction: Roth, Bellow, Updike. I wrote it, and was pleased with it; but I could never publish it without infringing the copyright owned by the Tolkien estate, and so it will languish on my hard drive until the world it describes comes out of copyright, 70 years after the 1972 death of Tolkien himself.

3 Mary Shelley's *Frankenstein* is acclaimed by many as the foundational text of modern science fiction. It has frequently been reworked and reimagined, modernized and adapted. There are, it seems to me, more and less imaginative ways of doing this. The less imaginative include things like simply relocating the 1818 European story to a twenty-first-century American setting, while the more include Brian Aldiss's brilliantly bonkers time-travel fantasia *Frankenstein Unbound*. I've always itched to write my own sequel to the book. You'll remember that, in the original novel, Frankenstein creates his monster and is then prevailed upon by the lonely creature itself to fashion a mate. Anxious that the monster would otherwise destroy his own private happiness, Frankenstein relocates to Ireland and builds a female monster. But at the last minute he has second thoughts, and tears his creation to pieces instead of animating it. What would have happened, I wonder, if he had gone through with his original plan? The monster promised to take its bride and travel to the New World. I like to imagine it did so and the two hideous creatures lit out for the territories of the South American Amazon basin. I once began to plot out a sequel, set in Brazil in the late 1950s among fugitive Nazis and Fortean explorers, while legends of a race of supermen hidden deep in the jungle were being proven true.

4 *George Orwell's Nineteen Eighty-Four* was one of the books that had the greatest impact on my young mind. The story Orwell tells is of the struggle of a compromised but heroic individual against the oppressive might of the totalitarian state. But I have often wondered whether it would be possible to write the story in a more *Antigone*-like manner (see above!) – a more balanced account of the world of the text. What might the novel look like from O'Brien's point of view? What if the physical hardships

61

Orwell describes so vividly were removed and everyone in his state enjoyed physical plenty and mental variety. Is the horror of the story less that of living under totalitarian tyranny and more the inconvenience of material deprivation? Another idea: O'Brien insists he is working towards the elimination of the individual, for a world where only states have existence and their citizens are no more than the atoms that make up those entities, as our cells make up our bodies. What if he and his kind succeeded? When the literary estate of George Orwell comes out of copyright at the end of this decade, I might write *Twenty Eighty-Four* (or *1984 A Century Hence*) – a novel in which it is the states themselves who are the characters, not individual human players. What might such a world look like? What if aliens came to the planet not in 1950s America but to such a world?

5 **The Invisible Man/Woman.** Of course, you're already familiar with the two most influential versions of this idea – *The Invisible Man*, H.G. Wells's fable of a nasty-minded scientist who invents 'invisibility' and then uses it to try to gain wealth and power for himself by evil means; and Tolkien's *The Hobbit* and *The Lord of the Rings*, where a magic ring grants first Bilbo and then Frodo invisibility. But how would it actually work in real life, being invisible? Our eyesight works because the light-sensing cells in our retinas send impulses to our brain, which converts them into images; a perfectly transparent retina would be perfectly useless. So, assume that the technology, or magic spell, turning your character invisible also renders him/her blind. How does that affect the story? Under what circumstances would it be worthwhile making somebody invisible if you were thereby blinding them? (For example, say you're a government agency or an army and you want to send in an invisible spy to recover useful information: could you recruit people who are already blind and know how to find their way about the world? Would you have some kind of sonar equipment for them to wear? Would your invisible person have to memorize their route ahead of time, blindfold? What would happen if the location into which they were inserted changed?) Also, is the 'invisibility' technology or spell reversible? If not, what goal could merit permanently blinding someone?

Inventing story ideas (II): the swivel

Writers sometimes have to generate ideas for individual commissions, where the parameters are specified. This, though, is a particular version of a more general problem: writers have to come up with ideas.

Take a premise, a generic tag, a general idea – like a subgenre (zombie stories, vampire stories, alternative history, the alien encounter, the quest) or one of the popular props or tropes of science fiction and fantasy more generally (the time machine, the robot, the ray gun, faster-than-light travel, the magic ring, the knight-in-armour). Or, maybe, take a simple feature of the universe like its enormous size, or the fact that it is expanding, or the nature of entropy. Now make a story idea out of this.

What I'm asking you to do, in effect, is to pick up the idea (do so metaphorically: I would not advise you to try *literally* picking up an idea) and look at it from every angle. Hold it in your hand and turn it, swivel it, upend it.

Think of something so basic that everybody takes it for granted. Then ask: 'What if this were the other way about?'

Here are a number of story idea exercises, derived from turning, upending and otherwise swivelling conventional SF and fantasy tropes. At all times, when considering a story idea, you should be asking yourself: What's the dramatic potential here? Where is the conflict? You can hold that in your head by means of the following: 'Always be asking yourself: what's the dramatic potential here? Where is the conflict?' This is the handy mnemonic: ABAYWTDPHWITC? (This mnemonic also doubles as a name for a villainous alien or goblin.)

We live upon a finite planet, and that planet exists within an infinite universe. This is only common sense. But what would it be like to live upon an infinite planet within a finite universe? If your initial reaction to that is to snort – impossible! – and dismiss the idea, then (a) stop snorting; it isn't becoming and (b) think again. Christopher Priest used this simple, brilliant conceptual inversion as the basis for his 1972 novel *Inverted World*. You can read the novel and see how he worked out all the details and implications. Be assured: it is a masterpiece of twentieth-century science fiction.

Greg Egan wondered what the universe would look like if, instead of possessing three spatial and one temporal dimension, it possessed four fundamentally equivalent dimensions. He published the resulting 'Orthogonal' trilogy from 2011 to 2013.

What if gravity suddenly switched through 90 degrees? The flat earth would become an endless vertical cliff face; most people would fall off, though some might survive – but what sort of life would they live? How would they cope?

This 'inversion' strategy need not be limited to the content of your stories. You can play similar games with the form, too. I once wrote a novel called *Yellow Blue Tibia*, set in the Soviet Union and Ukraine in the 1980s. It is about UFOs, the legacy of Stalin and governmental conspiracies and all that kind of thing, and I wanted to write it as an exciting action-adventure story of the James Bond or Bourne mould. But before I started, and to try to avoid producing a sort of plastic copy of a tale that had been told a thousand times before, I made a quick mental checklist of the sorts of things that invariably appear in those sorts of spy-adventure yarns, resolving at every point to do the opposite and see how it panned out. Since the hero is generally a virile, handsome and young-ish man of action, I made my hero an elderly, frail, ugly and cranky SF writer. The heroine is generally a toothsome young lingerie model whose main pastimes are looking pretty and getting into trouble so that the hero can rescue her. Accordingly, I made my heroine a highly intelligent, morbidly obese American Scientologist visiting Moscow. That's content, but I also thought about form. A standard action adventure will involve a succession of chase/fight action sequences, building in intensity towards a climactic bang-bang-bang conclusion. I decided, therefore, to write my novel with the big explosion (the 1986 detonation of the Chernobyl nuclear plant, with my hero inside it) in the middle of the book. The challenge then became: how to make the love story between hero and heroine feel real (which turned out to be easier than you might think); and how to be able to carry on the second half of the story after I had blown up an entire nuclear power plant with my hero inside it.

Inventing story ideas (III): lateral thinking

Story ideas can come from simply teasing out, or otherwise thinking through, the implication of a popular phrase, saying or book title. For example: let's say I have set myself the task of writing a story with the title 'Long Time No See'. It would be a story about seeing, or more specifically about blindness, or about characters who were blinded a while ago and who are now seeking revenge. Why and how were they blinded? Because I'm a science-fiction writer, I might think: through some form of research or advanced technology. I'm going to go with: a group of government agents agreed to have their optic nerves fitted with special transmitters so that everything they see is beamed straight back to Langley HQ. After a mission of particular sensitivity, three of these agents have code fed back to these implants that disables them, rendering them blind. 'An accident', their superiors assure them, as they are invalided out of the service. But *they* suspect the order was given deliberately, to prevent them seeing something. But what? And how far can three blind men get, pitted against the entire US secret service?

I can feel the story juices starting to come together, actually.

Titles can provide similar prompts. Wells's *War of the Worlds* is a classic of the genre. What might comprise a story called 'Oar of the Worlds'? How might an 'oar' function on such a scale? Not a literal sculpted plank of wood, of course, but something that could propel or steer the passage of an entire world? Some kind of hyperspatial projection, or quantum field generated and shaped via the high-energy flux and pressure of the planetary core? Who would have control of such a thing? How might they use it? (There would be no need to write this story as a pastiche of Wells, although you could if you wanted to.)

Snapshot exercise

Giving yourself no more than three minutes for each of the following, take the phrase and jot down what story ideas they give you. Note (a) the basic idea for the story; (b) the mode, tone and scope of the story (science fiction or fantasy? Serious or lighthearted? Long or short?).

- A Stitch in Time
- The (Square) Root of all Evil
- The Four Thousand Horsemen of the Apocalypse
- Time Flies
- Ignorance is Bliss
- The Whale at the World's End
- Paradise Frost
- Pig in a Poke
- To Be, Not to Be, Or Some Third Option
- The Wizard of Was
- We All Live in a Yellow Space-Marine
- The Hunting of the Quark
- Nerds of a Feather
- Carpe Noctem
- Moby Dick and Moby Jane See Moby Spot Run

Inventing story ideas (IV): the mash-up

I'm relegating this to last, since it seems to me a clumsy and often barren mode of 'story idea generation'. At the same time, I cannot deny that publishing and Hollywood have been cranking the handle hard on precisely this machine for the last couple of decades. Take a popular idea or trope (let's say: *Jaws*-like shark adventure); take another popular idea or trope (zombie stories). Put them together, and ... presto! Zombie Shark! (Out of the brine, hunting for brains!)

Yes, well, so: that's the problem, right there. There is too often something cheesy about the result of this story-generation strategy: *Pride and Prejudice with Zombies*; *Snow White Meets Godzilla*; *Fifty Shades of Gandalf the Grey*; a school for vampire wizards; a steampunk *Star Wars* – and so on.

Yet it wouldn't do to be too dismissive. The principle here is one worthy of holding on to. Sometimes two ideas are mashed together to produce only a clumsily welded derivative doubleness; but sometimes (to appropriate Oscar Wilde) two ideas are combined to produce – a star! Examples might include Disney studio's decision to combine *Bambi* and Shakespeare's *Hamlet* and so make *The Lion King*; or the Wachowski brothers' inspired combination of *Neuromancer* and kung-fu B-movies into *The Matrix*.

Summary

Cool premises and ideas, the high-concept zinger, the brilliant conceit – these are at the very heart of science fiction and fantasy. This chapter has grouped story-inventing strategies into four broadly conceived groups:

- *Clearing the decks*
- *The swivel*
- *Lateral thinking*
- *The mash-up.*

What these all have in common is a getting into the mental habit of taking often over-familiar ideas and rotating them, metaphorically, so as to examine them from every angle. Sometimes ideas arrive out of the blue sky, and that's wonderful – but you can't necessarily depend on that.

Where to next?

To repeat myself from the previous chapter, the overarching project is for you to at least map out and ideally to draft a complete novel. Now is the time to settle on a central idea for your story. If you haven't thought of one that really grabs you yet, then go to SF Plotto at the end of this book and choose one from there. What we're going to do in the next chapter is sketch out the larger shape of this idea, and (in the chapter after that) plot the whole thing out scene by scene.

4

How to structure your story

This chapter is going to introduce you to some widely practised rules of story structure. In keeping with the 'You need to know the rules – but only so that you can break them!' ethos of this book, I'll note straight away that there are *many* different approaches to structuring a novel. Any structure that works is a good structure. But I'm also going to suggest you steer clear of a common attitude to structure found in genre writing. Viz:

Something awesome happens on every page!

'I have read stories that start with a fight scene, move on through three set-piece fight scenes interspersed with dialogue and travel, and that builds up to a huge boss-level climactic fight scene. I want to write a book like that because fight scenes are dramatic and exciting!'

'Dude? That is *so* underpowered. I'm going to write a 300-page book that is one long fight scene – because fight scenes are dramatic and exciting!'

'If one man shooting a gun is exciting, then eighty men shooting eighty guns must be eighty times as exciting!'

Well, no. I can go further. Very much no. It will not surprise you that I say: no. Less is more. If everything is turned up to 11 all the time, the result is cacophony. Not that I have a problem with cacophony in its place – it can be a very effective aesthetic strategy, if used sparingly. But all cacophony all the time is just monotonous – and monotony is the worst sin a novelist can commit.

A single gunshot going off, after a long period of tense build-up, is exciting. Sitting inside an oil-drum for three hours while people outside hit it repeatedly with bats and drop firecrackers in at the top is just wearisome. That's because it's not the gunshot that is exciting: it's the interplay between the tension and its release.

This is perhaps a greater danger for science fiction and fantasy than for other modes, because a larger proportion (by no means all, though) of our fan base consists of youngsters and teens. And there is a widespread prejudice against such people that they get bored quickly, and so their attention must be continually engaged with bright colours and flashing lights. This is, I think, untrue as an observation about young people; but never mind that for a moment. Let's agree that your job as a writer is to engage your reader's attention (always think of a single reader, not a mass 'audience', because books and stories always have to do their job on the level of individual people reading individual books). 'Engaging your reader's attention' means not letting them get bored. It means making them want to keep turning the pages or flicking the corner of the e-reader screen. They may do this because they really really want to know what happens next; or they may do this because they have surrendered their imagination to the world of the story and are caught up in its flow – because they prefer to be inside the story than out in the world.

If 'what happens next' is always BANG! BANG! BANG! then readers will grow bored.

But by the same token, the world of your story need not be 'happier, brighter, more wish-fulfilly than the real world' for your reader to want to go there. This is just one of those oddities of the human condition. Sometimes readers are looking for a mental vacation in the broad sunlit uplands; but often they are happy to swim down into misery, to yomp through the metaphorical brambles, to parch in the metaphorical desert.

I'm going to illustrate this point with two quotations from Chandler. Anyone who can write a novel as taut and effective as *The Big Sleep* and *still* be able to say all those witty things on *Friends* has got to be worth listening to.

Here is one of Chandler's most famous quotations, a kind of summary of his career as a writer: 'The demand was for constant action; if you stopped to think you were lost. When in doubt, have a man come through a door with a gun in his hand.' Of course: for 'gun', here, read 'quantum teledisruptor'. Or equivalent.

There are two things to note regarding that quotation:

1 He is saying, when the story sags, have a man come through the door with a gun in his hand. He is not saying fill your story with an endless succession of men coming through the door with guns in their hands.

2 He is not offering a general rule for good writing; he is reflecting on the constraints of writing hard-boiled crime stories during the Depression. Actually, to read Chandler is to see that he understands something crucial to good writing – shooting a gun is, in story terms, the least interesting thing you can do with it. A gun is much more powerful, dramatically speaking, *before* it is discharged.

Here is a rather more eloquent Chandler quotation about a gun, from the end of *Farewell, My Lovely* (1940):

> *I needed a drink, I needed a lot of life insurance, I needed a vacation, I needed a home in the country. What I had was a coat, a hat and a gun. I put them on and went out of the room.*

Here the gun is a symbol not of empowerment, masculinity, exciting or bang-bang-bang. It is, on the contrary, a token of everything Philip Marlowe lacks in his life. The things we have make poor story material. The best stories are about what we lack.

Your job as writer is not to give the reader what she (thinks she) wants. Your job is to hold what she wants in front of her face, like a donkey's dangled carrot, so that she shakes herself into motion and progresses through the story after it. This is your job because, whether she realises it or not, your reader doesn't actually want the carrot (the macguffin, the solution to the mystery, the defeat of the Dark Lord). What she wants is to be in motion.

Write flash fiction

Here's another timed exercise in writing – one hour, as many words as you can type (you should be able to type at least 750 words, and probably more, in 60 minutes). As before, don't overthink this, and aim for flow. If you find yourself flagging, try free-associating, simply putting down whatever thoughts are roiling in your head. Turn on the radio and write down whatever the announcer happens to be saying, and then follow it on, turning it into the texture of your story. Whatever you do, keep going.

The purpose of this exercise is to imagine a Bang!-Bang!-Bang! event or device, and a person who desperately wants to push its big red button (or whatever) – and then to find ways of postponing that catastrophe. It doesn't matter what ways you find: a hero to thwart his dastardly plans, a sudden access of conscience in the main character's mind, a need to wait for the right time. Write the story so that it is oriented towards an ending in which the disaster will be set off.

When you have done this, set it aside. And when you come back to it, see how it would work either with or without the disaster happening at the end.

The three-act structure

You have an intriguing and original premise for your story or novel; and you have identified where the 'conflict' or 'drama' is. Now you need to think about how to structure your story. You will have a number of core characters (one, two or three; you can have more if you like but it gets hard to juggle them all. Better, usually, to have one, two or three core characters and as many subsidiary characters as you need for the story). You will have a sense of what your starting point is, and where you need to get to and you will have a sense of the main plot points you want to hit on the way – the big set-piece scenes, the twists and reversal and reveals. If you don't have those things in mind, then you'll need to get them.

Right away, though, you can see why the 'three-act structure' is so popular with writers. The basics you need to have before you can start are already more-or-less disposed into it. This is also why 'trilogies' are such a popular mode in fantasy and science fiction.

In its simplest form, the three-act structure is beginning, middle and end.

THE BEGINNING

The beginning should set the scene, introduce your characters, and give your reader just enough sense of the backstory and what is at stake to make her feel invested in what follows; but not so much that she feels bored and clogged with detail. The way to do this is to give your reader the necessary information *via* some interesting event or development. The beginning is your story, or your novel's, launch-pad: set your protagonist a problem, and make it active – s/he has to do something, uncover something, create or destroy something

H.G. Wells, *The Discovery of the Future* (1901)

'The past is but the beginning of a beginning, and all that is or has been is but the twilight of the dawn.'

There are exceptions – *The Lord of the Rings* starts very slowly; a leisurely description of an old man's birthday party; a lengthy conversation between a wizard and a hobbit about the past; a slow walk from home into the new lands. Nothing bang-bang-bang happens until well past page 100.

THE MIDDLE

The middle should develop your story and your characters, moving them through the curves of your plotting while building the reader's investment in the world, and excitement about what is going to happen next. This latter will be easier to do if your readers care about your characters and what happens to them. It's common to make this development 'rising action'; your protagonist's attempts to resolve the problem set up in the first portion of your story have brought them to a crisis point – either they have resolved the problem only to find that the resolution leads on to larger, more challenging problems; or else they have failed to solve the problem and been brought low. Why must it be this way? Because if the problem is resolved straight away the story has come to an end. I'll repeat myself: the trick you need to acquire as a storyteller is not giving your reader what she wants – or, more precisely, holding off giving your reader what she wants without annoying her.

The events leading up to this midpoint have, by challenging your protagonist, caused him/her to grow as a person. This is what is sometimes called 'the character arc', and it is one of the things many readers go to stories for. Personal growth can't happen without setbacks; the cushioned and eternally comfortable life does nothing for the soul. Why do we fall, Master Wayne? So that we can learn to dress in bat-themed black fetish gear and roam the city at night. Without the fall, our character is merely a boring rich guy hanging out at the yacht club.

The reference to 'trilogies' up there highlights one issue with the 'middle' portion of your story: the main danger it runs is sag. Genre fans call this 'middle book "bridge" syndrome'. Or maybe they don't – I try not to speak to genre fans. But it identifies a real issue about structuring one's story. It's common sense.

The first book, or the first part of your novel, sets up your world, introduces a compelling conflict or problem; the third book or part of your novel contains the answers to the mysteries, the resolution of the plot, and often includes a big smash-bang denouement set piece. But what about the middle? Surely it is nothing more than treading narrative water? Nothing more than a conduit from the intriguing beginning-bit to the exciting end-bit?

In fact, the middle section is not a problem but a powerful opportunity. If you follow the conventional model, it will be the act in which your protagonist is temporarily defeated, in which s/he fails or is otherwise knocked back. Characters failing are almost inevitably more exciting than characters succeeding. Success simply stokes the ego; failure brings the whole gamut of personality into play, and the mettle with which a character faces failure is much more powerful and inspiring than the fist pumps and whooping with which a character greets triumph.

If you make your middle section about character it will, ideally, help the reader care more about what happens to him or her in the final act.

There's a reason why fans love *The Empire Strikes Back* more than *A New Hope* or *Return of the Jedi*; and it is not unconnected with the fact that it's that much more downbeat, that much more interested in the way its characters fail.

Graham Greene

'*A story has no beginning or end: arbitrarily one chooses that moment of experience from which to look back or from which to look ahead.*'

THE END

But all things come to an end, and so must your story.

Endings are hard. The conventional wisdom, as far as this is concerned, is that your story's end should pay off the readers' earlier investment in the story: it should set out the resolution of the story and its subplots. The ending should be climactic, screwing the drama to a pitch of excitement.

There are two problems that present themselves straight away here. One is the technical challenge of it: bringing all your plot strands into a satisfying resolution, upping the excitement level of your writing and so on. But there is a second, deeper problem, which focusing on these technical aspects serves, broadly, to ignore. That is that there are no endings in real life. Isolate any event as 'the end' and you must acknowledge the fact that life goes on.

Strictly speaking, there is one ending in real life and it's called death; but that is no use to us, narratively speaking, for the following reason: when it happens to somebody who is *not* you, life goes on; and when it happens to you it's all over; so there's no post-death perspective from which you can look back and assess the shape your story took overall. You may believe in an afterlife; but if you do you'll probably agree that what comes *after* life is radically different from life, and so of very little relevance to it, narratively speaking. Ethically speaking is another matter. And if you don't believe in an afterlife, it brings us back to the core observation: if you are in a position to be able to look back and judge the shape of your life story for its elegance, effectiveness and so on, well, then, your life story is still going on and its shape may be subject to further changes. The most we can do in real life is take temporary stock.

This is important for the storyteller, since stories that depart from our instinctive sense of how life actually works will feel, to one degree or another, false, shrill, hollow or straining for effect. This is something of which science fiction and fantasy writers need to be *more* aware than writers of realist or mimetic fiction, for obvious reasons.

Structural variations

Right: let's tear that model up, remembering at all times that whenever we tear we want to do so in interesting and productive ways. Break any story into its three stages, and then think: what happens if we move things about? What happens if we divide the story differently?

For example: what happens to your story if you reverse the three-act structure? The climax will come at the beginning (so hopefully keeping your reader interested) but she won't properly understand it until we get the backstory and premise in the final act. How do you keep a reader reading if she is baffled by what's going on?

For example: let's take the classic alien invasion story, *The War of the Worlds*. The way H.G. Wells wrote this describes a broadly three-part shape. The first two parts have a good deal in common with the standard 'Hollywood' model for the larger story arc.

1 The coming of the Martians – the first intimations that alien life exists and is interested in us; the arrival of the alien craft; and humanity's first responses.

2 The Martians attack. Humanity suffers a major setback – the alien weapons are far superior to ours, and they sweep all before them.

How to carry the story through? One way (again, I don't mean to pick on any particular Los Angeles suburb, but we might think of this as the 'Hollywood' arc) would be to follow the 'downstroke' of Act 2 – humanity brought to the edge of defeat – with an 'upstroke' Act 3 in which humanity, perhaps inspired by our hero, rallies and strikes back against the aliens, destroying them, perhaps by capturing a piece of Martian technology and turning it against the invaders. But Wells decides to take the narrative in a different direction.

3   The Martians consolidate their hold on England, enslaving and devouring humans; our hero is driven underground in desperation. It looks increasingly as if the world is doomed, until – at the last moment – the aliens reveal a susceptibility to earthly viruses, against which their Martian existence has provided no immunity. The aliens die and humanity is left to pick up the pieces.

Tolkien coined the term for this: 'eucatastrophe', he called it. It's the very last-minute swerve away from the heartbreakingly tragic ending. But as you can see, Tolkien didn't invent the idea of the eucatastrophe.

One of the reasons it works as well as it does is that readers know the shape of stories already. We have read so many of them, or at least have seen so many TV and cinema versions of them, that we are all conscious or unconscious experts.

Snapshot exercise

Pick one of the following well-known stories, fables, people or events and sketch out its three-act shape. This might be: premise/conflict + downturn + upturn – but it might be any other three-act structure that seems to you to give a satisfying shape to the material.

- 'Little Red Riding Hood'
- *Beowulf*
- World War II
- Adam and Eve
- The discovery of a new land, or world
- The life story of Marie Curie, or Abraham Lincoln, or J.R.R. Tolkien, or Nelson Mandela, or Moses.

Workshop

Back to your proposed novel. The exercise now is to write an imaginary review of this work. The review should be 200–500 words long, and should give your prospective reader (a) a sense of what the book is about, and (b) an idea of what is so good about it.

'Imaginary reviews' are a genre in their own right: Borges and Stanislaw Lem both wrote many of them. They are a useful way of getting an overall sense of how you want your finished story to look. You can, in your review, stress both the good and weaker qualities of the imaginary work – just as real reviews do. This is a handy way of flagging up strengths and weaknesses to yourself.

Summary

This chapter has been about the larger structure of your story, with an emphasis upon the three-act structure. Three is not a magic number, of course; you may find a larger conception needs a more Shakespearian five-act structure (but you will tend to find that Acts 2–4 become an extended middle act); and for short stories a one-act brevity may be needed. The purpose of this chapter, though, has been to get you thinking about structure in this larger sense.

Where to next?

Now we need to put some meat on the bones of this skeleton structure. The next chapter will be about plotting, and breaking your whole story into discrete connected scenes.

5

Storytelling

You have an idea. And you have a basic, three-act sense of how you plan to structure and develop that idea. Now you need to think about the actual storytelling.

By storytelling I mean the actual process of laying the story before the reader. This is more than just plotting. If all people wanted was plotting, we could dispense with these 1,000-page fantasy tomes altogether and sell one-page story outlines containing all the key plot points (perhaps after the manner of the hawkers of ballad sheets of old). Storytelling is the actual nuts and bolts of realizing your great idea. It is the rendering of a plot into actual words on a page.

This chapter is going to give you some pointers as to how to achieve this; but before it does we have to face one unavoidable fact. The best way to get good at storytelling is to tell a lot of stories – you learn by doing, not by making notes on somebody else's telling.

Philip Pullman

'After nourishment, shelter and companionship, stories are the thing we need most in the world.'

Storytelling is that part of the writer's art that keeps the reader reading. A story well told will hold the reader's attention. But there's a perhaps counter-intuitive corollary to that simple and obvious fact, and its one we've touched on before. It is that the best way to keep people interested is *not* to scream and yell in their face. It is not to cram every page with over-the-top incidents – explosions, gunfights, magic battles, sexy dances, titantic monsters more more more! One bomb going off is exciting; ten thousand going off is deadening and boring. In fact, we can be more specific: one bomb going off can be exciting; but the tense period of anxiety leading up to the detonation of the one bomb is much, much more exciting. This is what 'less is more' means. It doesn't mean 'I'm going to have a huge explosion on every page, but only write 200 pages instead of 400.' It means: 'I'm going to identify what the reader wants – the solution to the mystery, the threat averted, the two protagonists to fall in love and kiss – and then I am not going to give it to them for as long as I possibly can.' The longer you can hold out, without losing the reader's attention, the stronger the storytelling pull of your tale will be.

 # Key idea: 'Chekhov's Gun'

This is a phrase used to recall us to a narrative parsimony. If the early part of your story draws attention to something, this sets up a narrative debt that needs to be repaid later on. What the great nineteenth-century Russian Chekov actually said was, 'Remove everything that has no relevance to the story. If you say in the first chapter that there is a rifle hanging on the wall, in the second or third chapter it absolutely must go off. If it's not going to be fired, it shouldn't be hanging there.'

It's good advice, as long as you take it with one large granule of salt. The easiest way to pay off the narrative use of Chekhov's Gun is to fire it; but played right, and knowing that your readers will be expecting the gun to be fired, finding narratively satisfying ways of not firing it can be just as powerful.

Now common sense tells us that there will be a cut-off point, after which readers are going to start to say 'Wait … are you just stringing me along?' That's the last thing you want to happen. Readers want some kind of a pay-off, even if it is not necessarily the conventional or expected one; and if you frustrate them in this they will not love you. I'm not sure there exists a reliable algorithm for determining when this cut-off period is, mind you. If you start your fantasy series with the promise 'Winter is coming …' how many thousands of pages can you write set in late summer before your readers revolt? (Quite a few, it turns out.)

There's a related problem, too: if your story becomes overwhelmed by one particular deferred outcome, then it gets harder and harder to write the climax without engendering 'powerful anti-climax'. If everybody is expecting Ross and Rachel to get together, and that expectation is delayed year after year, season after season, when they finally do it the buzz will be brief, friable and cast a malign pall back over the fans' experience. Exhibit number 1 in this respect is the TV serial nonpareil of delayed viewer gratification, J.J. Abrams' *Lost* – and most especially the catastrophic levels of viewer anti-climax the last series of that show generated, precisely because it had done such a good job up to then of keeping its fans on pleasurable tenterhooks.

This latter dilemma is harder to avoid than you might think. One approach is to give the readers more than one story strand to be interested in, and not put all your story eggs in one deferment basket. And let me tell you: if somebody had told me, when I woke up this morning, that I would be sitting at my desk typing the sentence 'One approach is to not put all your story eggs in one deferment basket', I would not have believed them. It's a funny old game, writing.

This is advice that, clearly, applies to longer stories more than to shorter ones. So, yes: a longer story will be made up of several strands, braids, elements, storylines, whatever analogy you prefer.

As a rough rule of thumb, you should aim to keep the reader guessing about these on three different levels:

1 **On the level of base story** (the mystery, the threat, the drama inherent in your premise – will the Z-bomb destroy the world? Will the spell giving all men pig snouts instead of noses be reversed?).

2 **On the level of character** (what will happen to this varied and likeable cast of individuals to whom the story has introduced us? Who will live and who will die? Who will fall in love with whom? What secrets from whose past will emerge?). And ...

3 **On the level of reader expectation.** Readers are not fools. They have read a thousand stories like this before: they know that the Dark Lord is going to be defeated, the world saved, the guy get the gal; and on a formal level they know that the story will build through smaller reverses and mini-climaxes to a big Boss Level denouement climax. If you can inject uncertainty on this level, you will generate tension in powerful new ways. To take one contemporary example: George R.R. Martin is a master of this, and not just because he is happy killing off major characters at the drop of a medieval-style hat. His storytelling skill is much more technically accomplished than the simple random slaughter of individuals. What he does is play his storytelling along the groove of his readers' expectations, such that they think the story is basically about Character X, with all the other characters offering support. If you can sell your readers that dummy, then the sudden swift demise of Character X (at a wedding, say) does more than give your reader a short sharp shock. It destablizes her sense of what is coming next.

Here is some advice from the Victorians, whose best novelists were experts in the storytelling arts. Many novels were published in serial instalments, such that you would spend a small sum once a month for the latest packet (three chapters, say) of story about your favourite characters. It is a set-up critics sometimes compare to TV serials today, although Victorian novels usually tied up their story over 20 instalments, and so could not keep the narrative treading water for years and years as is the norm for successful television stories.

Wilkie Collins, friend of Dickens and a mean storyteller himself, had the following three pieces of advice for the writer of serial fiction. How should you treat your reader?

- Make 'em laugh.
- Make 'em cry.
- Make 'em wait.

This is good advice for today's storyteller. Let's break it down a little.

The first two are aspects of the same imperative: you must engage your readers' empathy where your story is concerned. Your readers must care what happens to the characters. A SF or fantasy world, no matter how ingeniously ornate and built, which hosts the stories of characters readers care nothing for is a barren text – a video game dynamic of flattened affect and monotony. But there's some point in breaking it down the way Collins does.

Laugh!

You don't necessarily have to write brilliant comic prose and have your reader hooting with laughter – but you do need to engage your reader with some species of positive effect.

There's a clear and present danger in some modes of dystopian and military science fiction, and in the grimmer, darker varieties of fantasy, that it can all be immensely serious and po-faced and earnest. That's a killer. Your storytelling needs humour and wit as much as it needs earnestness and grimness, and it needs those things because without them it becomes almost impossible for your story to connect with the readers. Maybe you *had* a miserable time at Suburbitown High School, and people mocked you for your geekiness and that girl/boy you had special feelings for wouldn't so much as look at you and broke your heart by dating that vacuous good-looker instead. I feel for you. I really do. But if your reaction to that is 'I have suffered so now I shall make my readers suffer, I fall upon the thorns of life I bleed and now you must weep!' – well, then you may find your readership disinclined to take that narrative journey with you. Your story need not be cosy, of course; and erring too far on the comforting side is, if anything, a worse error. But you will need to leaven your grimness and dystopian intensity. And when you do you'll find that, by doing that, you have found the magic ratchet that ratchets up the tragic aspects of your work.

So how to introduce the positive effect? The Hollywood cliché way is to give your noble and tragic main character a comical sidekick. A Sancho Panza. A Jar Jar Binks. Make your main character tall, attractive, brooding, driven and serious. Make his/her sidekick short, unconventional looking, bumbling, given to malapropisms or comic deflation.

This may work for you, but as with all cliché you need to handle it very carefully, with the tongs of creative reimagination. Better, I think, is to work the positive effect into the whole story; to keep a light touch on your prose; to make your dialogue witty and sprightly; to give all your characters, not just the sidekicks, actual human failings and warmth. Nor does your sidekick need to actually tag along to the left of, and three steps behind, your hero. Since I've mentioned George R.R. Martin once in this section, I'll mention him again, to observe that serious tragic hero Jon Snow and fan-favourite sardonically witty Tyrion Lannister fulfil this narrative role even though they do not, together, constitute a buddy-buddy team. And this example goes to show something else: if you write it well enough you may find that your readers start to consider the sidekick the main-kick, and your brooding Byronic noble hero becomes a more marginal figure.

Cry!

The essence of drama is conflict; and the way conflict works its way out in the practice of storytelling is by knocking back your protagonist, depriving him/her of the satisfactions they seek. When that happens to us in real life it makes us sad, and when it happens to characters we empathise with we experience a similar vicarious emotion. This is good. A good cry, and anybody who has had one recently will tell you, is cathartic (not me: I'm English. I cried once in 1981 for about a minute and a half, but not since. But other people will confirm this for you). And actual tears need not flow for the catharsis to be effected.

Howard Baker

'You emerge from tragedy equipped against lies. After the musical, you're anybody's fool.'

Kids understand this. Sometimes the reverses that afflict us are not fair. And, truly, 'That's not fair!' is a very potent emotional state to which to connect your readers. It's so potent, in fact, that you need to be scrupulous about paying it off at a later point in the story. If your tale says nothing else other than 'It's not fair – but, hey! Life's not fair! The universe isn't fair, get over it', then your tale will be a lunkish and ill-mannered thing. Maybe that's the kind of story you want to tell: that's up to you. But you'll find that a story that parlays its 'That's not fair!' into subsequent reversal and pay-back will win readers in quantities and with loyalties the lunkish story cannot match.

There's another kind of reversal, which, though painful, is kind of fair. This is the tragic flaw. This was an idea originally popularized by nineteenth-century Shakespearian scholar A.C. Bradley: that Shakespeare's greatest characters bring their downfall upon themselves. Othello is a noble, brilliant general and leader of men, but he is also prone to jealousy and that leads to his downfall and death. Macbeth is a brave, loyal soldier whose flaw is ambition. Hamlet is a sensitive, intelligent prince whose flaw is, um, wait: procrastination? Really? That's a character flaw now, is it? OK: not everybody agrees with Bradley on Shakespeare. But we can see the enduring dramatic appeal of the tragic flaw model. We all have a sense of our own imperfections. Could we really identify with and empathise with an absolutely flawless individual? Characterization (not to get ahead of myself – see below) means creating the illusion of human depth, and ideal perfection in a character would be perfectly depthless. Your clever, wise, capable, good-hearted hero/ine is more interesting if s/he also has a crippling gambling addiction. That then means you have to decide whether you want to play that flaw out into tragedy – in which case the flaw scuppers his/her best efforts – or into comedy. In the latter case your story will become about how s/he overcomes her flaw. That can make a good story too, although the risk you run is writing a feel-good, happy, hugging-and-learning upward trajectory story, and the problem with *that* is that it becomes banal. And you don't want to make your readers vomit with disgust at the wholesomeness and positivity, now, do you?

Deferral

There's one crucial way in which the instincts of a professional storyteller have been rewired from the instincts of a regular person storyteller. Of course, we are all storytellers, all the time: whether it's passing on gossip, or telling a joke, or coming back from work and unloading on our partners with 'Oh, what a day I've had ...!' But here's the difference. If something noteworthy happens to a regular person, they will tend to front-load that thing in their storytelling. If you had a small car accident on the drive to work, you'll tell people like this:

> *You'll never guess what happened to me today! I was involved in a car crash! Not a serious crash, I'm pleased to say – nobody got hurt, we're all fine, everybody exchanged insurance details and so on. What happened was I came to the turning on Winston Avenue and the lights were out. So I was inching out, waiting to turn left when this lunatic in a red Toyota came straight at me and smacked into my front bumper ...*

You tell the story this way because you don't want to leave your auditor in any anxiety about the outcome of the story – you're fine, no bones broken, the insurance will sort out the car and so on. This is perfectly normal and natural; no decent person likes to make other people anxious unnecessarily. Even the professional storyteller may relate his/her small traffic shunt in this manner to friends and family. But when it comes to structuring her story in a professional context, she would look at this and say: there's one tiny – though in its way still effective – delay in this narrative structure, and it comes after 'You'll never guess what happened to me today!' After that the story rushes with unseemly haste to satisfy the auditor's curiosity. It simply doesn't make them wait long enough. The next sentence 'I was involved in a car crash!' is immediately defused by 'Not a serious crash, I'm pleased to say – nobody got hurt, we're all fine, everybody exchanged insurance details and so on'. And in fact it comes already pre-defused by the 'I', since the auditor can see that the person telling the story is basically all right. This is one of the problems with first-person narration: the reader at least knows the narrator survives long enough to tell the story. Better, then, to shift it to the third person. And better to withhold from the reader the information that the individual survived unhurt, that the crash was easily resolved. Make the journey the protagonist was engaged upon vital – it's imperative s/he get to their destination, and fast! The crash interrupts this. Describe the crash briefly but vividly. Is the protagonist killed outright? No; but there's a high risk of injury. And now how will s/he get to her destination in time …?

In real life you aim to defuse anxiety. In your storytelling you aim to ramp it up. But it's OK because that's the metaphorical contract the reader signs with you when they pick up your story. You read a scary story to be scared. You read a creepy story to be unnerved. And you read any kind of story to be kept in a state of weirdly pleasurable anxiety about what's going to happen next, and how it's going to pan out …

Don't misunderstand me. There are many varieties of 'Wait!' Not all of these, and not the best, are defined by a crude and open-ended 'What's going to happen next?' metric. Indeed, you can achieve remarkable effects by playing around with this.

Punctuating the story from scene to scene

This 'scene' is the building block out of which the story is constructed. Once you've set up your premise and got the ball rolling narrative wise, the storytelling will consist in laying out a coherent sequence of scenes that are related to one another causally, and that draw the reader through the experience towards the conclusion. Or – not. I hate to repeat myself, but rules are nasty things. If you can construct your story so that the scenes do not follow causally from one another, or do not build according to the conventional logic, or any other variation you can think of – then bravo, brava, bravissimo. As long as your reader is engaged enough to keep reading, you have won.

But let's lay out a simplified skeleton model of the use of the scene in storytelling, either for you to follow if you like, or for you to subvert using your cleverness if you prefer.

Let's work with a notional novel-length structure: a give-or-take 300-page, 100,000-word novel. It starts with an original and arresting premise – your core idea for the story – and you have already thought about that premise and worked out where the conflict and therefore the drama is in that idea. You've also, as per the previous chapter, had a thought about the three-act structure that will give architectural shape to the novel as a whole.

For our purposes, each key scene in the story will be given its own chapter. It needn't be this way; you can work several scenes into each chapter if you like (though that may well mean that your novel becomes too busy, and feels clogged); or you may stretch key scenes over several chapters, by punctuating chapter endings with mini cliffhangers. But for our purposes let's stick to one scene per chapter.

There are no legally binding rules on how long a chapter should be; but a good rationale for breaking your story into chapters is the convenience of the reader. She will probably not read your whole 300-page novel in one go; and chapter endings make convenient places to pause. If your chapters are too short, you don't give your scene space to develop, and you give your novel an overall bittiness and staccato quality. If your chapters are too long, you may test readers' patience. Let's work with – again – a simplified template and say each chapter should be somewhere around the 5,000-word mark. That's the length of a mid-length short story, and it should give you the elbow room to hit the following storytelling hot points:

- To move the story on in a way that gives the reader a quantum of satisfaction while introducing a quantum-and-a-half of new 'Wait!' anxiety.
- To develop characters, or character interactions.
- To add an increment to the worldbuilding, not by simply dumping in salient features of the place but by integrating new knowledge of the world into the story – so that moving the story on and/or developing the characters happens via some new, relevant and cool feature of your imagined world.

In practice, 5,000 words is quite long for a chapter in a popular novel (you'll probably write more, shorter chapters), but let's stick with the simplified model for a moment.

You can do the maths: we're looking at 20 more-or-less equal portion chapters. That is to say: your story will express itself across 20 discrete scenes, each one interesting, engaging and onward-moving – although not all interesting, engaging and onward-moving in the same way. That would be monotonous. A proportion of these scenes may be bang!-bang!-bang!, but if they all are (or if your idea of variety is 'scene 5 will be bang!-bang!-bang! with a gunfight, and scene 6 will be bang!-bang!-bang! with hand grenades, and scene 7 will be bang!-bang!-bang! with laser cannons …') then the result will be a bored reader. Instead, aim for a ratio of three scenes in which the tension is increased for every bang!-bang!-bang! scene.

With a chapter at the beginning to get things rolling, and a chapter at the end reserved for post-climax wrapping up, that gives us a three-act structure disposed across 18 chapters: six chapters per act. If this seems a little too neat to you (and it may), then skew it towards the ending: say five chapters for Act 1, six for Act 2 and seven for Act 3.

Act 1 should have a clear storytelling direction, and should close with a narrative resolution that opens up larger vistas or more significant narrative 'Wait!' potential. Act 2 should follow through on these, and move the story up a notch, heading for its second mini-climax. This is the point at which the fullest implication of the premise first becomes clear to the reader, and will probably involve a large-scale setback for our protagonist.

Already we have broken up the imposing block of 100,000 words into more navigable shorter blocks.

Umberto Eco

'All the stories I would like to write persecute me. When I am in my chamber, it seems as if they are all around me, like little devils, and while one tugs at my ear, another tweaks my nose, and each says to me, "Sir, write me, I am beautiful."'

Let's work with a specific example – a notional novel I've just made up on the spot, to be called *Twelve Years a Robot*, or *12YAR* for short.

Pick an initial driver for *12YAR*: I'm going to suggest – kidnap.

Let's say *12YAR* is a SF fable, set in a world where computers and robots have taken over for mankind's own good. After a near-apocalyptic war, the AIs redesigned the world; now everybody has a house robot – actually their master, but treated as a beloved pet by the human beings. Your robot runs the house, handles all the family needs, and (in our particular story) manages the chronic radiation neoplasm disease that affects our protagonist. The only fly in the ointment is a criminal underground that steals robots and ransoms them back to families. The story starts when the robot goes missing; the protagonist approaches the robot police to help, but instead they turn on him/her and attempt to lock him/her up. S/he escapes by the skin of his teeth; but s/he must find his/her robot or the radiation disease will incapacitate and eventually kill him/her. S/he daren't go to a hospital for fear of running into the authorities. So s/he hires a human PI (and friends) to help him/her track down the robot. Act 1 of the story will be the search for the robot; and each of the five scenes will move the protagonist, his/her helper and any other characters you have assembled towards the goal of finding the robot – and it has to happen soon, or the disease will destroy him/her. In chapter 6 the kidnapper's lair is finally discovered and the robot is there. But there's a twist! Not only does the robot not want to be rescued, but it is in charge of the kidnapping gang!

Act 2 starts with the protagonist facing radiation disease collapse within a few hours; stripped of his helper and bewildered by the turn of events. Through chapters 7–12, the story moves to its second mini-climax, when our protagonist discovers the extent to which the AI (and its robots) are tyrannically ruling the world. Our friendly house robot seems hell-bent on destroying our protagonist, and his/her best plans are defeated. The second twist revealed in chapter 12 can be whatever you want it to be. Let's say it turns out that the robots are revealed to be the true humans – survivors of the war who uploaded their consciousnesses into these metal bodies in order to be able to survive the devastation; the 'humans' are clone-grown organic androids, soulless Turing Machines, being developed by one tribe of post-humans nostalgic for flesh-life, in the hope that one day they'll be able to upload their consciousness back into corporeal form again. The robots regard these flesh humans as pets, or experiments; and the radiation disease is actually a set of design flaws in the clone technology that they are trying to eliminate. The final Act, then, can lay out the implications of this story. Maybe the robot humans have lost touch with their essential humanity; maybe the clones have more integrity and individuality than the robots ever suspected. Our protagonist's house robot, apparently the baddie in Act 2, is revealed as the good guy after all – he experienced moral qualms at the way the cloning experiments were going, and took himself off grid the better to fight the powers that be. Together, protagonist and robot organize a rebellion against the powers that be, in order to ...

But you can see how this is going.

The crucial thing is that every single one of the 18 scenes of your 20-chapter story should contribute to the onward flow of the whole. Sometimes this will involve things happening. Sometimes it will involve revelations. But mostly it will involve making the reader laugh, and cry, and wait.

For example, in one scene, set your protagonist a deadline, and make it a tight one. Make sure that it's a meaningful deadline, with clear negative consequences if it is broken, and one where we as readers are invested in the outcome. Then, at the end of that scene, cut the deadline in half. The next scene could be your protagonist desperately trying to meet this new deadline. At the end of *that* scene, cut the deadline in half again. You're into the third scene – halfway through one of your acts – and nothing needs to have 'happened' for the reader to be galloping through your story with their tongue out. Metaphorically speaking.

Here are a few other dos and don'ts:

Don't keep chopping and changing the point of view (POV). It's fine not to want to stay stuck in a single character's POV the whole time. But signal the shifts clearly for the reader, and don't hop about between multiple characters within the same scene.

Related to this is the layer-cake principle of storytelling. It's common to end a scene on a cliffhanger, and then to shift the following scene to a completely different plot strand. The whole book can be layered this way; and in one sense it's easy to see the advantages – it means that the reader is denied the resolution to the cliffhanger that much longer, and has added thereby to the story's 'Wait!' quotient. But there are dangers, too. One is that the reader will resent being wrenched away from a plotline she was enjoying and was involved in – so the transition needs to be handled with some aplomb. Start the next scene with enough of a hook to make the reader want to plunge in. There's a related problem with the layer-cake structure, and it's that by redirecting the reader's attention you defuse the intensity of the preceding cliffhanger. Your reader *did* care about what was going to happen to character X, but now you've redirected her to character Y and the previous cliffhanger seems much less pressing.

Practicalities

One reason to try writing regularly is to try to create in your praxis a sense of the sort of through-flow you want the reader to get from the finished product. It's easier to do this if you write a thousand words every day for three months straight than if you write a little here, a little more three weeks later, a chunk a day for four consecutive days then nothing for a month and so on. Be, as they say, as regular in your habits as the bourgeois, the better to be able to produce the mind-blowing marvels in your work.

Part of this is simply committing yourself to the process. Writing is the long haul. As with anything, you get results by applying yourself regularly over a long period of time.

But I'm going to assume that you are committed. So maybe the problem is to do with the roadblocks you encounter on the way. You set time aside each day, but you want to use that time actually writing, not staring at the blinking cursor on a blank screen. Writers all hit roadblocks at one time or another: you simply can't think what to write next, where to take the story, how to go on.

 H.G. Wells

'There comes a moment in the day when you have written your pages in the morning, attended to your correspondence in the afternoon, and have nothing further to do. Then comes that hour when you are bored; that's the time for sex.'

Don't panic. Here are five roadblock tips:

1 **Leave the house.** For many writers, the ability to work from home is one of the big advantages of the gig. Not I. My problem is that there are too many distractions in the home – too much housework that still needs doing, too tempting a TV set in the sitting room. My solution is: I get out of my house. In fact, my routine is doubly constrained, since I have kids and a day job. But on the days when I don't have to go to actual work I drop the kids at school and go straight thereafter to a coffee shop. I buy the largest mug of coffee the shop sells – under UK tax law, and according to my accountant, this is a deductible expense – and write until I have drunk it all. Other people sometimes look at me askance, as if to say, 'Oh, you're *pretending* to write a novel are you? You poseur!' But I am proof against their silent scorn. Because I know that I actually am writing a novel.

2 **Film yourself.** Some people recommend this if you are blocked or having trouble working out a problem. My Plan A solution in such circumstances would be: just write – start writing, and see where it goes. But a Plan B is to use your webcam, or set up your phone, to film yourself – and then simply talk. Explain the problem to yourself and chat through possibilities. You may feel a little foolish, talking to a computer; but there's no one else around. And for some people the novelty of this, or the shift in mode from writing to talking, unlocks solutions.

3 **Write something else.** If you're having difficulty working through a difficult passage, try, try again – and then stop; there's no point in making a fool of yourself. But don't stop writing: write something else. Either a different section of the same novel/story; or something else entirely. You can always come back to the original point of blockage. Indeed, swapping your focus can be exactly the way to conjure a solution to whatever was blocking you before.

4 **Order is your friend.** The best way to write a novel is through regular habits. If you're writing in your own flat or house, tidy your workspace. Settle down to work at a set time, and work for a set length of time before breaking for lunch. Write lists and tick off items as you achieve them. If you're Monica from *Friends*, you probably do this anyway. If you're not, this may sound lame to you but, believe me, it works.

5 **Bribe yourself.** Promise yourself a prize or reward for hitting a certain word count, or getting to the end of each chapter. It can be chocolate, or a toy, or a half-hour break on the PS4 – it can be whatever works.

Workshop

Take the idea you have decided upon for your novel. Open a new file and create 20 numbered spaces – or, if you prefer to work by hand, get a fresh sheet of paper and number 20 slots. 1 is going to be 'Opening' and 20 'Conclusion'. Divide the remaining 18 into three lots (three blocks of 6, or one of 5, one of 6 and one of 7 – or any other dispensation you think would work for your story). Then sketch in each of the 18 middle scenes, using between one and three sentences per scene.

This exercise will take as long as it takes; but don't let it drag on. You can sketch out a story in an hour; if two hours have passed I expect you to have finished. Don't worry about getting absolutely everything finished and perfect – you are producing a working model, not a finished masterpiece.

Summary

We have developed the broader 'act' structure from the previous chapter with a finer-grained sense of the flow of scenes across a novel. We talked about dividing the larger three-act structure into 20 individual 'scenes' (a longer novel will need more scenes, a shorter one fewer; but we picked on 20 as an indicative example).

I propose three main principles for the structuring of a longer tale:

- *Make 'em laugh – the importance of human feeling and warmth.*
- *Make 'em cry – the astringent of suffering to wash away any banal sentimentality or cosiness.*
- *Make 'em wait – the central importance of deferral.*
- *We talked about punctuating the larger story in terms of specific scenes, using the example of a novel I just made up called '12YAR'. Yah!*
- *We finished with some practicalities.*

Where to next?

Now we come to some of the specifics of writing: how to write good rather than bad prose and believable rather than clunky dialogue. Descriptive prose and dialogue will almost certainly make up the lion's share of the book that you write.

6

Writing well: description and dialogue

It is probably fair to say that neither science fiction nor fantasy enjoy much of a reputation for stylistic excellence. There are some noted 'stylists' in genre, but the majority of writers aim for a functional tone rather than an expressive or poetic one. And there are plenty of writers – especially among those who self-publish or post their writing online – who are actively bad. This chapter will be about steering you away from bad writing and towards good writing. But before I can do that, I need to say what I mean by those two terms.

So this chapter will cover: what to avoid, stylistically; what to aim for in your style; how to write convincing, flavoursome dialogue; and some hints and tips to lift your style.

We'll start by defining 'bad' and 'good' writing.

The first is the easier of the two to pin down. Bad writing reeks with its own special stink, and you can hardly miss it. There are two main things to look out for: bad writing as simple incompetence, and bad writing as more complex overreaching, a failure of tact.

Bad writing as simple incompetence

Of the first kind of bad writing, we can say these three things:

- **Bad writing is ungrammatical.** Maybe you feel yourself to be a rebel, a Joyce, somebody to whom the rules don't apply. But you can't break the rules if you don't understand the rules and most of the time those rules will inform everything you write. Your sentences should contain at least a subject and a verb, which should agree in number (so 'the alien battleship were larger than the moon' is ungrammatical). Don't slide queasily from past tense to present and back.

- **Bad writing is poorly punctuated** – use full stops at the end of your sentences; be very sparing with exclamation marks and never use more than one at a time!!! STEER CLEAR OF SHOUTY CAPITALIZATION! It looks foolish and immature – and beware the excessive use of *italics* for *emphasis*, because *like capitalization* it *very* quickly becomes *annoying*. Don't keep changing your font, just because there are a thousand different fonts available on your computer: it doesn't look lively and emphatic, it looks lame and distracting. Don't underline things.

- **Bad writing is poorly spelled.** This is more than just using your computer spellchecker to make sure to get your 'i-before-e-except-after-c' ducks in a row. It means getting clear in your head the difference between 'your' and 'you're'; the difference between 'its' and 'it's'; the difference between 'who' and 'whom'. (This latter seems to puzzle a lot of people, although I've never understood why – everybody understands the difference between 'he' and 'him', or 'she' and 'her', after all; and it's the same distinction being drawn. Would you write a sentence like 'She gave the ray gun to he'? No. No, you wouldn't.) If you think these sorts of things are pettifogging and pedantry, then you're in the wrong business. Using language correctly is the baseline skill upon which all other writerly achievements – including those that muck around with the conventions of language for comic or experimental reasons – are built.

In all these things, your best guide is the good practice of writers you admire. Not all published writers exhibit good practice in all this, but the overwhelming majority do, not least because their work has been through the filter of error-correcting editors and copy-editors.

Your best ally is a willingness to get it right. I'll be clear: it is possible to believe, as many people do, that the 'rules' of grammar are arbitrary constructions, and that they are changing under the influence of things like text-speak. Once upon a time, writers all sounded like Dr Johnson. It's possible that in the future we'll all write like LOLcats. People who study grammar insist that their discipline is *descriptive* not *prescriptive*; that they're not laying down unalterable commandments. As a general attitude to language use, this seems to me quite right. As a strategy for improving your writing, though, it is less helpful. Working through 'rules', however arbitrary, is a way of forcing yourself to think about your own writing practice. Learning how the rules work is the necessary first step to knowing how and when you might want to break those rules.

I'll give you a couple of examples of what I mean. You may have heard the following 'rules':

- Avoid split infinitives.
- Use the subjunctive for an unfulfilled wish or condition.
- Never end your sentences with a preposition.

The interesting thing here is that plenty of people, including esteemed linguistic and grammar experts, would deny that they are 'rules' at all. People break all three and are still readily understood by others – and that, surely, is the crucial test of communication. When William Shatner speaks his voice-over segment during the *Star Trek: The Original Series* credit sequence, claiming that their five-year mission is 'to boldly go where no man has gone before', we understand him even though he has split his infinitive. People all the time say 'If I was ...' ('If I was going to write a novel, it would definitely be about a telepathic brain slug') without being misconstrued – even though the grammatically correct form is 'If I were ...' And as for ending sentences with prepositions: well, structuring your sentences so as to avoid ending them with prepositions ('to', 'of', 'with' and so on) very often results in forced and artificial constructions. Winston Churchill famously mocked the kind of person who insists upon this grammatical rule: 'This,' he declared, 'is the kind of thing up with which I will not put.' Implicitly he was saying: but *surely* it feels more natural to write 'This is the kind of thing I won't put up with.'

But here's the thing, for me at any rate: 'This is the kind of thing I won't put up with', though communicative, strikes me as bland, whereas there is a rather splendid elegance in the supposedly mocking 'This is the kind of thing up with which I will not put.' The advantage of writing with a sense of the rules of grammar in your head is that it often forces you to think more carefully about what you want to say than might otherwise be the case. The point is not blindly to follow the rules; it is to think about what you want to say, about how you want to arrange your words, and about the effect you are going to have. Language is not a transparent medium through which readers will view the motion picture running in your head. Language is the material out of which the artwork is made.

Bad writing as overreaching

But there is a second aspect to bad writing, and I need to spend a little more time upon it because it is so rife in science fiction and fantasy. It is, indeed, so common that we even have a shorthand for it. That shorthand is 'Thog'.

'Thog' is a barbarian warrior, whose taste in 'differently good' writing is the subject of its own annex on David Langford's long-running and multiple-award-winning fanzine *Ansible*. You can find out more about the sentences from science fiction and fantasy selected for Thog here: http://thog.org/

Thog's tastes are not as other people's. The sort of writing that brings his barbarian sensibilities pleasure are of this kind:

Rod's eyes broke away from the ghost and wandered
slowly about the great chamber.
Christopher Stasheff, *The Warlock in Spite of Himself*, 1969
Jack pulled back his fists in readiness, and eyed the druid
through clenched teeth.
'Maze', *Pro-Am: The Serial*, 1999
Kothar leaped, leaving his booted feet and diving a yard
above the floor ...
Gardner F. Fox, *Kothar – Barbarian Swordsman*, 1969

You get the idea. Many more of these can be found on Langford's site, and all from published works (a fact which I, as a writer, find heartening: after all, if this rubbish could get published, then how much better the prospects for my own much better writing!).

I'd say Thoggisms fall into two categories. On the one hand are the symptoms of incompetence where a writer has been so caught up in their writing that they fail to see how ludicrous what they have said is. On the other are sentences that simply strain too hard for effect. I'll give you an example:

Sex, like a thousand-headed snake, wound its dark coils
and convulsed in agony, tightening upon the conflagration
[in the hero's soul] and concentrating its malevolence
and potency, pulsing the hellish plasma to new levels of
atrocious ferocity.
Colin Kapp, *Transfinite Man*, 1964

Key idea

Damon Knight coined the phrase 'gingerbread' to describe a particular kind of bad writing – for the sort of writing style that trades in useless ornament, such as 'fancy sesquipedalian Latinate words where short clear English ones will do'. Bad writers are tempted to 'gingerbread' in 'the hope of disguising faults and conveying an air of refinement'.

Here's another example: R.S. Johnson's *The Genesis Project: The Children of CS-13* (2011), a book which stands pretty much in its entirety as an object lesson in how not to do it.

101

But Zuberi did not see this, nor did anyone else, and as he
slid his pistol back into its holster, the main door
to the room flew open and about a dozen men
and women, who had been sleeping only
moments earlier, poured in, their weapons held and
ready to fight if need be, a few more arrived soon after.

Afterthoughts are jotted down in this manner all through this novel,
just as the stream-of-writerly-consciousness disposed them. And now
there they lie, in the finished and printed book: trapped like hairy
Jurassic bugs in the amber of the writer's disinclination to revise.
The lesson to be learned from this is: *revise.*

Or:

The blue carpet underfoot was embroiled
with the CyberTech Defence Systems insignia
every five meters or so.

The lesson here is: you keep using that word. I do not think it means
what you think it means.

Or:

'The first move has been made,' he said, not
tearing his eye from the body.

That's 'eye', singular.

Or:

As the droplets became heavier as they fell upon
his body as he walked towards the car, Elliot
began to laugh in fits of hysteria.

There's something hypnotic in the repetition of all those 'as' clauses.
I rather wish the writer had expanded the number to more than
three. Fifteen might have been good. Or a hundred. Then there's:

The island was actually made up of three separate parts.
One large, classed as the mainland, and two smaller.

But if ...? No, wait. What?

Robert mouthed the word 'I'm so sorry,'
before disappearing into the crowd.

The news helicopter slowly circled, showing the United
States Embassy in its awful reality.
But before Mark could reply, there was an awkward
clearing of a throat.
The room was monumental. Brightly lit from above, the
entire screen was filled with row upon row of rising blue
fabric chairs, all of which were occupied by both men and
women, young and old. They were all staring down at
something and a moment later a majority showed stern
expressions and were shaking their heads.
He tried to remember how many rungs there were,
but with his brain bearing this gravest of news
and him wondering whether this ladder would still
hold his weight, it was impossible to remember.
He knocked several times at the door in a sort of rhythmic
fashion, pushed it open and crawled through.
Finally the Genesis Project like a ball of string was
beginning to unravel itself!
A single walnut door stood either end of the long,
grand hallway.

Examples are reputed to work more forcefully upon the mind than
exhortation. Let these examples work upon yours.

What is good writing?

This is a rather harder question to answer than 'what is bad writing?'.
In part, this is because it can be answered in a number of different but
equally valid ways. For some people, 'good writing' means a stylistic
richness and vividness, a lyrical polish and fineness to the prose. For
other people – and especially in science fiction – this is merely over-
writing. Such people believe that a writer ought to avoid purple prose
and concentrate on being expressive, clear and direct.

Is your ideal stylist Updike or Hemingway? Nabokov or Alasdair
Maclean? There's no right answer to this question.

Vladimir Nabokov

> *'I automatically gave low marks when a student used the dreadful phrase 'sincere and simple' – 'Flaubert writes with a style which is always simple and sincere' – under the impression that this was the greatest compliment payable to prose or poetry. When I struck the phrase out, which I did with such rage that it ripped the paper, the student complained that this was what teachers had always taught him: 'Art is simple, art is sincere.' Someday I must trace this vulgar absurdity to its source. A schoolmarm in Ohio? A progressive ass in New York? Because, of course, art at its greatest is fantastically deceitful and complex.'*

To dilate upon this for a moment – I'm trying to be even-handed – a 'clean' prose style is, I'd say, more favoured in science fiction and fantasy than a 'fancy' one. And there are some good reasons for it. The main one, I'd say, is that readers generally find it easier to engage with clear, straightforwardly expressed writing, and may be put off by the effort required to navigate fancier styles. I say this not to denigrate the capacities of readers (in my experience, SF and fantasy readers are smarter and quicker on the uptake than the average Joe or Joanna). It is to speak to a fundamental feature of genre writing.

The argument goes like this: science fiction and fantasy are both, fundamentally, about things that aren't in the world. We are already expecting our readers to navigate strangeness. A strangeness described in a clear style is one thing; a strangeness described in an estranging style is a strangeness too far.

I understand that reasoning, although I don't (personally) agree with it. The way it seems to me, prose should always be more than just a functional content delivery system. It should be a pleasure in itself, such that every single sentence should provide – and irrespective of what information it conveys – joy. Nabokov thought the real business of a writer was bliss, and that's not something you can do by content alone. For me, 'plain' prose is often grey, flavourless and dull prose.

But this is not a matter upon which I can hand down tablets of graven stone. Your fundamental duty as a writer is to commit to writing well – but you first have to decide what constitutes good writing for your story.

That said, there are a few things that are transferable between the different modes:

- **Avoid cliché:** As the old joke has it, you should avoid cliché like the plague.

- **Every sentence counts:** Don't think in terms of 'filler' passages that lead up to a killer moment; and don't think that one special well-turned sentence justifies a certain proportion of dull work. Pay attention to everything you write. Readers read your work one sentence at a time, and that's how you should write it.

- **Aim for elegance:** Clunky, over-obvious phrasing is bad' whether you're aiming for plain or purple style.

- **Aim for restraint:** Many of the 'Thog' phrases listed above are evidence of writers desperately striving for intensity, or to avoid cliché. You need to develop a sense of writerly tact, to be able to judge which new-minted ways of describing things, which metaphors and phrases, work – and which are ludicrously over the top. This is as much a question of reading the phrases in their context as judging them on their own merits.

- **Ration your adjectives and adverbs:** This is probably the most common error I find in the beginning writing I teach – and it's not limited to newbies. Some writers think that piling on the descriptive modifiers makes writing more lively and imaginative. It really doesn't: it clogs. One of the most useful exercises you can undertake with your first drafts is to go back through them crossing out almost all of your adjectives and adverbs. It's an idea to set yourself a limit – one adjective per sentence, for instance. It's a good rule of thumb that the need for an adverb is a signal that the original phrasing was not precisely chosen enough. You don't need to write 'he walked slowly' when you can write 'he strolled'; you don't need to say 'he said furiously', or 'she exclaimed sarcastically' if you have written the actual dialogue to convey those qualities. Adjectives, similarly, are like salt. Used sparingly they add flavour to description; overused they render it very rapidly unpalatable. Which of these two sentences seems to you better?

> *The Sky-rider strode up the hill where his dragon waited for him under a blue sky.*

> *The Sky-rider walked quickly up the steep green hill towards its broad flat summit where the golden-scaled, black-eyed young dragon was waiting patiently for him to climb into the elaborately tooled, luxurious, red-leather saddle and fly into the clear, inviting, cloudless, azure sky.*

- **Avoid clumsy repetition:** I find this is one of the tasks of revision: during composition the brain, tired or overtaxed, often reaches for the same word. Revising my manuscripts is very often a process of spotting repeated words, and either cutting, reconfiguring the sentence or finding a synonym.

- **One exception – 'said' is fine:** The truth is that 'said' is more textual placeholder than word; it is there to let the reader know that characters are speaking, and as such has almost no flavour. For much dialogue you won't need to use it at all, but when you do stick with 'said', don't feel the need to keep modifying it to 'screeched', 'hollered', 'whispered', 'muttered', 'bloviated', 'harangued', 'drummed', 'barked', 'whinnymongered' or any other such nonsense synonyms.

- **Vary sentence length:** This, again, is something easier to judge when revising your work than when first-drafting it; avoid great stacks of same-length sentences (especially great stacks of short sentences), and don't let your fancy-pantsness skill with long, spooling sentences clog up your reader's passage through your story.

- **Show, don't tell:** So vital a principle of writing is this that we devoted a good chunk of the first chapter to it – on the grounds that a particularly toxic form of telling-not-showing called 'infodumping' is particularly rife in genre. But it bears repeating. So I'm repeating.

Writing about tech

Not all science fiction includes tech, but a lot does. The watchword here is non-splurge. Do not splurge. You may be terribly excited by all the intricate knobs, flywheels and flashing lights of your item of imagined technology. That's nothing to be ashamed of. But your reader is more interested in what the item of imagined technology does and means, not how it works. I can be more specific: most readers feel this way. There are some readers who will share your geeky fascination with blueprints, scale models, instruction manuals and so on; but they will not be the majority. When your Techjammer books have become so mega-successful that your fans number in the millions (most agree that *Techjammer 5: Pro Game on Proxima* is the best) and your publisher is begging you to write a book called *Jam On: The Official Companion to the World of Techjammer* – well, then you can indulge yourself. Fill a whole book with specs and plans and describe every last nut and bolt. Until then, remember that your tech exists in your story to serve that story, and must be subordinate to it. The same applies, *mutatis mutandis*, to fantasy. Your job, in the first instance, is to write your *Lord of the Rings*; it is not to write your *Appendices to the Lord of the Rings*. Your job, of course, is not to write anything so derivative as your version of *The Lord of the Rings*. It is to write your own fantasy. But you take my point. I love the appendices to *The Lord of the Rings*, and have spent many happy hours browsing them – but it's a love subsequent to and predicated upon the love I have for the novel itself.

There is a sweet spot when it comes to the description of tech, between too much clogging and story-slaying detail on the one hand, and too vague and hand-wavy an insouciance on the other. Your readers need to know what your tech does and how it affects your characters and story, and that means that they need to believe in it.

For example, let's say your story involves a time machine. Filling seven pages with a welter of specific technical detail will only bore the reader: she is not interested in your four-dimensional flux capacitors, the rotating quantum gyroscope fitted behind the field buffer or the Cherenkov pile situated in the main roll-bar. But she needs to know *something*. Saying 'Ronan's time machine was a three-metre high silver egg powered by Magictrons' will leave her tut-tutting.

There are two distinct issues here. One is actual tech – which is to say, pieces of kit extrapolated from established principles that could work if only they were built. This is the minority of SF tech, but it's a significant part of it. When you're writing this, be sparing with the details. The rule of thumb is: the more pleased with yourself you are about your ingenious new way of constructing a space plane, laser rifle or robot, the less specific detail you should include.

Two is bullsh*t science tech. Here, there is no 'actual' scientific underpinning, and the job of the writing is to give your account the patina of plausibility. It doesn't have to actually make sense; it just has to sound right – and it has to sound right enough for the reader to buy into it, so that it can advance the story and add to the roundedness of the characters.

This means jargon; and good jargon is a skill in its own right. There are dangers here. Generating jargon about a technology or aspect of science you don't really understand can produce results to make readers wince (it's like young kids trying swearing: they sort of know the kinds of things entailed, but their swears never sound quite right). There are problems with short shelf life, too. Few things date more catastrophically than period-specific jargon. Partly this is because, over the last 50 years, tech has moved so rapidly it's been hard to grasp it at any one point (think of *The Simpsons'* Professor Frink in 1970s threads and hairdo, standing before a room-sized computer and announcing proudly: 'In twenty years these machines will be five times as big and almost 50 per cent more powerful!') But it's often because writers pick up a contemporary buzzword and then toss it carelessly about. I remember watching an episode from the old 1930s movie-serial *Flash Gordon* where one character declared histrionically of the hero: 'His brain has been infected by radiation! He'll descend to the level of a brute!' Something similar will doubtless obtain in the future when readers look back and see what we did with 'quantum'.

Getting jargon right is best achieved through a kind of ventriloquism. Read actual descriptions of equivalent tech, not for the specifics but to get the flavour of the way it is being described – the sorts of idiom deployed.

As with description more generally, the way to steer past mere infodumping is not simply to describe your tech for the benefit of the reader but instead to use a description of the tech to move your character or story on in some salient manner. Which of these two ways of describing a mood organ do you think works better?

1 'First developed in the 2050s, the function of the mood organ was to adjust the balance of happiness and depression in the human brain in order to achieve levels of contentment that enabled people to get through their working day in a more productive and happier mode. This 'well-adjusted' sensation lasted up to 24 hours in most subjects. The machine worked by focusing quantum-shaved radiation at the frontal lobes. Dorian, like most people, used it soon after waking every day as part of his morning ritual. One day ...'

2 'The first intimation Dorian had of his brain tumour was when the mood organ began giving him headaches. He'd used the brick-sized machine as part of his getting-ready-for-work routine for years, and it had always adjusted his inner emotional turmoil to a fair approximation of contentment. But now it was also leaving him with a steady pain just behind his forehead.'

Your reader is thinking: 'Tumour! How will Dorian cope with *that*?' and as she reads on she has absorbed the nature and functioning of the piece of tech without even being aware that she has done so. The shorthand for this mode of writing is the *finesse*. It's a fine thing, the finesse.

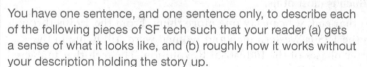

Write: tech description

You have one sentence, and one sentence only, to describe each of the following pieces of SF tech such that your reader (a) gets a sense of what it looks like, and (b) roughly how it works without your description holding the story up.

- Time machine
- Genetically engineered animal
- Matter transporter
- Futuristic weapon (of whatever variety you like)
- A pillow containing electronics that fill your dreams with transcendence
- A spaceship that alters the geometric co-ordinates about itself in order to shift space and so travel faster than light.

One more thing on tech

Tech is important. One of the ways science fiction works is by mediating the tech revolution that has determined human life for the last couple of centuries. That's a pretty sweeping statement, I know, and it has some important if perhaps counter-intuitive consequences. We live lives so saturated with high-tech machinery that it's easy to become blasé about it, or even blind to it. Tech makes our lives richer, but it also generates anxiety – when the mere thought of leaving the house without having your mobile phone with you gives you heart palpitations, then you know something's wrong. Tech makes us anxious because we don't understand it; we fear what it can do when it goes wrong because it reveals our inadequacies and magnifies our secret phobias.

Tech in SF stories will resonate most potently if it connects with this anxiety. If your tech is just an ingenious piece of kit, the most it will do is make your readers think, 'Well, that's pretty cool', which is one step along from 'Meh'. But if your tech connects with some subconscious anxiety, it can symbolize something important about our lives. Cyborgs in fiction resonate with readers to the extent that they articulate our own senses of the exhilaration and anxieties that we have all become cyborgs already – not just the people with pacemakers and artificial arms, but the people who can't leave home without their mobile phones and who spend all day on a computer. Which is most of us.

To that end, we can say one more thing. From the 1930s through to the 1950s Western men and women were still living in the latter phases of the Industrial Revolution. The tech that impacted most forcefully on their lives and therefore on their imaginations was *big*: bridges and cranes, giant planes and big ships. This in turn informed a mode of science fiction crammed with gigantic spaceships, moon-sized space stations, Godzilla-sized monsters and the like.

That's all great; and one advantage of big is that it touches on the logic of the sublime that in turn can generate a sense of wonder. But the fact remains: from the last decades of the twentieth century and through into our present twenty-first, the tech with the most forceful impact on our lives and therefore on our imaginations is not really the 'very big'. It is the technology of computing, data processing and, above all, of social interaction. This has tended to be small and getting smaller; but the salient point here is its logic of interconnectivity.

This isn't to say that you have to write about ultra-miniature kit, or invent a sort of Super Twitter ('Thritter! It's one step beyond Twitter ...'). But it does mean that the tech in your story that is liable to connect more forcefully with your readers will be stuff that connects with their sense of the way tech mediates their being-in-the-world. If your hero goes to work in a crowded office located in the head of a mile-high mountain-levelling robot[1] – well, that's quite a cool idea. But it won't trail fingers of dread across the tender membrane of your readers' imagination the way tech will that symbolizes (say) what it's like to feel simultaneously crowded and desperately lonely; to feel that you have no secret spaces left in your psyche; to have your very thought processes reduced to building-block slots of tweetable data.

Writing magic

Almost all the magic in fantasy novels is a wish-fulfilment exaggeration of specific human powers. The ability to read minds is an extension of normal human empathy; the ability to move things by thought alone is a refined version of our power to move things by picking them up; and so on. Badly written, this shrinks magic back into the disappointments and ordinariness of the mundane.

Arthur C. Clarke once said that any sufficiently advanced technology would be indistinguishable from magic; but that doesn't mean that when you write magic you should think of it as merely a kind of extra-advanced tech. If your story involves wizards with the ability to shoot shards of glittering lightning from the end of their wands just like guns, then you might as well be writing a story about people fighting with guns.

A reader in the year 1590 would be astonished at the Mages capable of communicating instantly over great distances. A reader in 2015 will be less impressed by this ability, seeing as how she carries in her pocket a device capable of precisely this that she uses many times every day. A Palantír seems less impressive in such a context.

You need to treat the magic in your writing less instrumentally. What I mean by that is: don't think of magic as a way of getting this or that done, as an instrument for achieving a particular goal. That may be part of the way your magic functions in your story, but it mustn't be the primary one.

---

1 'Mount-Down: North America's Premier Mountain Reduction Corporation. Is a stretch of high terrain spoiling your view of the sea? Do you need a flatter road to work, or a space cleared for a sports pitch? Or do you simply need millions of tons of rock-rubble for a building project of your own? Call Mount-Down on Free-Mob 7777. Our mile-high robot can be at YOUR eminence in a matter of hours.'

The reason you have magic in your fantasy at all is in order to evoke the numinous in the minds of your readers. Your magic should be uncanny, potent, eerie, discombobulating, thrilling. It should cost, and the cost should be proportionate to the strength and effectiveness. It should create a sense of wonder, of transcendence.

 C.S. Lewis

'The great value of myth is that it takes all the things you know and restores to them the rich significance which has been hidden by the veil of familiarity.'

The feeling I am talking about has been one of the main fascinations of post-Romantic art. Wordsworth called moments when he felt this almost luminous intensity, moments when the hairs would tingle at the back of his neck and his stomach curl in on itself in thrill, 'spots of time'. James Joyce called them 'epiphanies'. Both these writers wrote their own autobiographies (Wordsworth's *Prelude*, Joyce's *A Portrait of the Artist as a Young Man*) not as narratives of conventional happenings – being born, going to school and university, getting married, having kids and so on. Instead they told their lives as a string of high-point 'spots of time' or 'epiphanies'. This is what the magic in your fantasy should aspire to.

It is a feeling akin to religious transport, and you may want to conceive of it that way. I suggest this without intending disrespect to the many people for whom such feelings are profound and holy. I do so only to note that the interstices of your novel should have a god-ish quality that touches and moves the reader. I'm using 'god', there in the sense that Aldous Huxley defined it, back in his 1931 essay 'Meditation on the Moon':

> *'How shall we define a god? Expressed in psychological terms (which are primary – there is no getting behind them) a god is something that gives us the peculiar kind of feeling which Professor Otto has called 'numinous' (from the Latin numen, a supernatural being). Numinous feelings are the original god-stuff from which the theory-making mind extracts the individualized gods of the pantheon.'*
>
> Huxley, *Music at Night and Other Essays* (1931; reprinted London: Grafton 1986), pp. 60–61

For Huxley this 'numinous' feeling is a core aspect of the healthy psyche. It is not an argument for or against the actual existence or non-existence of a divine being; it speaks rather to the psychological make-up of the human animal. And it's this you should be working towards in your fantasy.

How? For this you need to look inside yourself, and note what it is that generates these moments of specific intensity. One of Wordsworth's insights is that his 'spots of time' are not connected with the conventional 'grand moments' in his life, but with occasions that seem almost trivial: waiting on a windy hillside for the coach to take him home after school had broken up for the Christmas holiday; walking in the Lake District and seeing the old remains of a prison; rowing himself across a lake as a boy and seeing the hill on the far side appear to rise up as he approached it.

This is true to how life is: moments strike into our soul at strange and apparently inexplicable moments. Try to determine what it is that gives you this access of intensity – this numinousness; and then work out how to roll that out across your fantasy world.

Writing fight scenes

It is the fate of writers of science fiction and fantasy to be more often in the position of having to describe combat than any other kind of authors, with the exception of thriller and adventure-yarn writers. There is a particular discipline to writing good fight scenes, and we'll touch on it here. But there is a particular trap many writers fall into also, and since it speaks to a larger problem with science fiction/ fantasy I'm going to start with it.

It's video games.

Many writers drawn to science fiction and fantasy are gamers. There's nothing wrong, of course, with enjoying video games. But gaming makes a very poor template for the writing of combat (or, indeed, anything else). Video game fighting is externalized, fiddly and intricate, more like a series of ballet moves than combat. Scenes based on having played such games read like this one, which is excerpted from an actual published novel, the title of which, to spare its author's blushes, I shall withhold:

> *He saw the opening and threw a brutal fist at it, low and*
> *under her nearly unbreakable ribs. She accepted the fist,*
> *twisting to mute it, felt pain blossom inside her as he*
> *connected. She planted a leg behind his knees and slammed*
> *her other hand into his shoulder to bring him down. Sam's*
> *booted foot flashed out. He parried the elbow, fell back*
> *and bent his leg to take her kick on his thigh instead of*
> *knee. Her body came all the way around, free hand lashing*
> *out in a palm heel strike to break his nose and drive the*
> *shattered fragments into his brain. The CIA agent dodged*
> *the strike with a preterhuman twitch of his neck.*

The author, here, has thought through the ins-and-outs of his
fighting carefully, and scrupulously lays them all out. But the result
is an inert piece of writing, one that fails to come alive. Here, by
way of comparison, is a description of a fight by a real master of the
form – Raymond Chandler. Here a character gets punched in the
1939 short story 'Pearls Are a Nuisance':

> *He snorted and hit me in the solar plexus. I bent over and*
> *took hold of the room with both hands and spun it. When*
> *I had it nicely spinning I gave it a full swing and hit myself*
> *on the back of the head with the floor.*

Because it takes you a moment to orient yourself with respect to
what's actually being described, this is prose that reproduces the
experience of being blindsided by a punch. And because it focuses on
the way the experience feels to the participant, instead of standing
outside the action relating it to a third party, it connects much more
powerfully with the reader.

Violence is not a ballet. It is intimate and terrifying; it leaves
you with persistent after-effects of panic and irrational fear. It
violates you (hence the name!). When you write a fight scene, pay
attention to the actual costs, both physical and mental. One person
punches another in the face. The puncher will at least bruise
their hand – they may dislocate their knuckles and render the
hand useless for days. (I once sat with a man who had just come
from a bout of bare-knuckle boxing; both his hands were like
purpled-pink irregular sacks of swollen skin, with each knuckle a
shallow granite thorn. He couldn't so much as hold a mug of tea.)

The person punched will also suffer: a hard punch to the nose is extraordinarily debilitating – it's not just the pain, it's the snorting, sneeze-spasming disarrangement of the sinuses, the blinding agony of broken nasal bones, the snot and blood. A punch to the eye might temporarily (or permanently) blind your character; the area will swell shut in minutes. A punch to the mouth might break a tooth, exposing the nerve – one of the single most debilitating agonies it's possible to experience. If your character is a 'tough girl' or 'tough guy', they might be able to override their pain and distress and keep fighting, although with reduced efficiency. But it won't last long.

Now, maybe that's not what you want to write. Maybe you're happy writing a video game fight scenario. That's fine: write what you like. But check your own instincts, too. What is it that appeals about such a scenario – a 20-minute elegant kung-fu dance? Is it the grace? Or is it, rather, the implied invulnerability? Because if it is the latter, and your real fantasy is to be the sort of person unbothered by pain, then that's what you need to be exploring in your writing. A wish-fulfilment fantasy in which anxious, timid 'you' is recast as Slugger the Space Pirate, who has walked cockily away from every fight in every low-down Asteroid Bar he's ever found himself in – Jack Reacher in space – then that's more or less banal. The drama in your writing is in the fear, not in the attempt to pretend the fear isn't there.

Similes

Used sparingly, a good simile can lift a piece of description; and when writing science fiction or fantasy – when, that is to say, you are describing things that may have no corollary in the real world – it's especially important. You compare the thing you are writing about to something else in a way that makes it come alive for the reader.

The key with writing a good simile is hitting the sweet spot. On the one hand, if you invoke only conventional and obvious comparators for your subject ('she was pretty as a picture, with an hourglass figure and dynamite hips') then you are merely perpetrating cliché. The image will remain inert upon the page. On the other, if you overreach yourself by using only the most outlandish and bizarre comparators, the results will be baffling, or ludicrous, or perhaps both. Many Thoggisms are generated exactly that way: 'Marty managed, winching his eyes like injured climbers around the dangerous overhang of her torso and up to the relative safety of her face'; 'She pouted, her lower lip projecting like the bottom drawer in a chest of drawers which has jammed open on account of too many clothes being stuffed inside'; 'His hand quivered his gun like an angry bush in the wind'.

At the same time, a good simile is worth its weight in diamonds. A well-chosen comparator can lift a piece of prose, driving a vivid or powerful image deep into the reader's imagination. So potent can the genuinely original simile be that it must be used sparingly, like strong spices in cooking, for fear of overwhelming the reader. It's the opposite of a cliché.

Vladimir Nabokov was a master of this kind of thing. His 1935 novel *Invitation to a Beheading* is set in a scrupulously realized run-down and shabby future world. One of the characters looks at the photographs in an old magazine and marvels at the splendour of twentieth-century existence – so graceful, so potent, so fluid! In each of the similes used in the passage below, Nabokov is estranging the familiar in order to bring it more forcefully back upon our imaginations, so that we see perfectly mundane things – a woman diving into a swimming pool, a high-jumper in mid-jump – in a new light. And this (to go back to Chapter 2) is precisely what science fiction should be in the business of doing!

> *That was a remote world where the simplest objects sparkled with youth and an in-born insolence, proceeding from the reverence that surrounded the labour devoted to their manufacture. Those were years of universal fluidity; well-oiled metals performed silent soundless acrobatics; the harmonious lines of men's suits were dictated by the unheard-of limberness of muscular bodies; the flowing glass of enormous windows curved around corners of buildings; a girl in a bathing suit flew like a swallow so high over a pool that it seemed no larger than a saucer; a high-jumper lay supine in the air, having already made such an extreme effort that, if it were not for the flaglike folds of*

his shorts, he would seem to be in lazy repose; and water
ran, glided endlessly; the gracefulness of falling water, the
dazzling details of bathrooms; the satiny ripples of the
ocean with a two-winged shadow falling on it.

Vladimir Nabokov, *Invitation to a Beheading*
(English translation by the author, 1959)

Overuse of this kind of writing can be problematic – the judgement
being one of taste as much as anything else. John Keats thought
the business of a writer was to 'load every rift with ore', as if sheer
bling were enough to make prose rise and fly. But – I refer the
gentle reader to the first chapter of this very volume – less is almost
always more. Say you come to a point in your story where you
need to describe a cruise ship at anchor in a bay at night, while
searchlights sweep the water. Which of the two following passages
seems to you better – that is, more effective, more fitted to the
moment?

1   He leaned against the rail, and watched the beams of searchlights
    sweep the black water, while across the bay a brightly lit cruiser
    rode at anchor.

2   At night, on board ship, he watched the empty white sleeves of
    searchlights filling in and sinking again across the sky, while the
    black water looked varnished in the moonlight and farther away,
    in the night haze, a brightly lit foreign cruiser rode at anchor,
    resting on the streamy gold pillars of its own reflection.

That last is Nabokov again. I love Nabokov with a passion, but even
I wonder sometimes if he goes too far.

Making similes

How to arrive at the perfect point of comparison? The best way is
to stop a moment, and think about the object or person you want
to describe. I mean, really think: try to defocus your mental image
a little and put aside all the conventional or clichéd comparators
('black as night, black as pitch, black as ink...') and try to fit a new
image to the subject ('black as liquorice, black as a berry, black as
the pupil of an eye ...').

Anthony Burgess had a trick which I'm going to pass on to you. Sometimes inspiration struck, and exactly the right simile occurred to him as he was writing. But sometimes he would stall and then what he would do was open his dictionary at the word he was trying to describe ('storm', say; or 'knife'). Then he would let his eye slide across the page, perhaps on to the next page, until he found a word that worked, that clicked with him as a vivid simile – staircase ('the waves rose in ragged stormy staircases towards the clouds ...'). As this trick, if overused, will tend to produce more than a pleasing proportion of alliteration, Burgess would leaven it by picking suitable words from the definitions of headwords rather than the headwords themselves.

Write some similes

Using the trick described above, find original and novel similes to describe the following:
- a *Saturn V* rocket
- a man riding a horse
- a smooth pebble
- white cliffs
- the Sun going behind the Earth's rim, seen from space
- a flame
- a sword.

Spend no more than one minute on each of these.

Good dialogue

It's easy to write good dialogue – so easy that the overwhelming preponderance of bad dialogue in science fiction and fantasy starts to look wilfully perverse. With bad dialogue, every character sounds alike, and everybody speaks to other people only in order to convey important plot points and to move the story along. In bad dialogue, people use cliché all the time.

In good dialogue, each character has their own distinct idiolect and sound; good dialogue is a mode of characterization as well as a way of putting story-relevant information down on the page. Good dialogue is a joy on its own terms. You want your dialogue to have specific flavour and zip; and you don't want it to be like the too-often bland, whitebread version of dialogue found in many novels.

So how do you write good dialogue? By paying attention not just to what people are saying but how they say it. Eavesdrop on people. Make notes. Read your own dialogue aloud, testing it on your own ear. Do people ever actually speak like that?

If you pay attention to actual speech, I think you'll notice two things – in writerly terms, they represent a DON'T and a DO:

1 People hesitate, um and err a lot more in speech than they do in novels. Don't reproduce this – it is tedious and draggy to have to, er ... you know, like ... to have to wade ... through, er ... um, through *dialogue* that tries to reproduce all the hesitations and repetitions of actual speaking.

2 Actual speaking has a rhythm and timbre to it all its own. Do try to capture this in your own writing.

It is a question, in essence, of writing out the content of the dialogue necessary for your scene, and then scratching and distressing it a little, stonewashing it so that it has the appearance of having been actually used. This is a trick: simply putting down verbatim speech on the page somehow doesn't create the right effect. You need to work towards the way language in everyday usage shifts, moves, pulses and fuses in unexpected ways

As an example of what I'm talking about, look at the following lines of speech lifted from various different places in Don DeLillo's 2004 novel *Falling Man*:

• 'I'll quote you that you said that.'
• 'She's got a great body for how many kids?'
• 'They put son of a bitches like you behind bars is where you belong.'
• 'I'm a person if you ask me questions. You want to know who I am? I'm a person if you're too inquisitive I tune you out completely.'
• 'Which is the whole juxt of my argument.'

This is great writing, with an almost poetic apprehension of the way throwing ordinary rhythms slightly off kilter can generate little jabs of beauty. The second one is particularly lovely – 'She's got a great body for how many kids?' – its jaunty knight's-move shape; that little bounce in its middle. Language in use, slightly scuffed and distressed but polished, shining (like the toe of a brass statue of a saint that has been touched and touched by decades of hands). This is more immediate, more corporeal, and tuned to the rhythms of lungs and tongues than is the typical, polished literary-boilerplate style. This is what you should be aiming for. Is the whole juxt of my argument.

I'm not suggesting that all your characters should sound like they've walked off the pages of a DeLillo novel. Far from it! DeLillo's characters speak like contemporary urban Americans, because those are the people he writes about. Your characters need to sound like themselves, however they are constituted. Every time they speak – excepting only the designedly terse articulations of 'Yes', 'No', 'Huh?' and so on – the way they say what they say should tell us something about them, just as the content of their communication conveys whatever it conveys. Dialogue should sound right, and chime in the ear when you read it aloud. You should aim for it to be a joy.

If your work affects a quasi-historical form, then you'll face the historical dialect problem. If the characters in your medieval-Europe-with-dragons-and-ice-zombies world speak the way actual people spoke in medieval Europe, then your readers are going to be left scratching their heads. There's only so much 'Quoth anon, worthie knight may haf it? Ye shall leave it youndre as Nacien þe hermit, shal be put aftre his death; for thither shal þat gode knight come the fifteenth daye after þat he shal receive the order of knighthoode: and so at day that they set is this time that he have his shielde, and in the same abbey lieth Nacien, the hermit who vaniseth awaye, by the grace of God, shall be wel set in me' that most readers can stand.

The best bet with this sort of dialogue is to aim for a fairly neutral, plain style into which readers can read their own sense of the time. Generally, you should aim to pitch into that safely neutral place, halfway between 'prithee my lord thou'rt in excellent fooling' on the one hand and 'we is in your base killin your doods' on the other – picking a path between that Scylla and Charybdis of contemporary fantasy.

Workshop

I want you to take another step in your ongoing novel and write a chapter. Pick any scene: the opening one if you're most comfortable doing that, or any of the later ones that sound intriguing. Then, without overthinking it, write the chapter. You should be aiming to do the following:

- End up with a finished but rough draft. We will be coming back to this draft later on, when it's time to talk about revising.
- Flex your writerly muscles with respect to both descriptive writing and dialogue. Keep in mind the points made in this chapter. Utilize some of the descriptions you jotted down during the shorter exercises we undertook through the chapter. Go!

Summary

This chapter looks at some examples of bad writing, and opens the question of what is good writing. But this latter question is so vast, and so central to the business of writing itself, that I could write 20 books on the subject and come no closer to an answer. All writing is the putting together of words to make stories, characters and worlds – and the best way to put those words together must be the continual focus and study of every writer.

We looked at some specific challenges the writer of science fiction and fantasy is likely to face:

- *writing about technology*
- *writing about magic, and the need to make your magic systems actually magical (tautological, I know; but you'd be amazed at how often the magic in fantasy novels comes over as dry and dull and mundane)*
- *writing fight scenes.*

Then we looked at the use of similes, and especially at the knack of writing original and vivid similes, pitched halfway between tired old cliché similes and bizarre random jolt-the-reader-out-of-their-reading-experience novelty similes.

We finished with a look at dialogue, and some hints as to the best way to write it.

Where to next?

The next chapter looks at character, and how to write it.

7

Writing character

For many readers, the real test of a great novelist or short-story writer is how she writes character. Your story will have major characters (perhaps one single main character, perhaps a couple) and minor characters. These will be agents in your story: you will need them to move around, to interact, to do stuff and discover stuff, fight stuff and make peace with stuff – whatever your plot requires. But if this is all your characters do then they will be flat and dull. They must act as well as react; they need to come alive on the page so that the reader remembers them when she has finished reading. A great character can carry a whole book.

There are particular problems, too, with genre writing about character. On the science-fiction side of things there is what we might, if we weren't worried about stereotyping fandom, call an empathy gap. 'Science' is a rational business, and many fans of 'science'-based narratives like things neatly and logically divided up. 'Character' (which is to say: human personality and subjectivity, all the stuff that makes individuals different from other individuals) is not a merely rational business. It is very far from true that all SF fans are Sheldon Coopers; but it probably is true that SF fandom as a whole skews a little further along the Asperger's spectrum than other groups of readers. There's nothing wrong with being a bit Asperger's, of course; and no reason why it should interfere with your ability heartily to enjoy stories and novels – but it presents certain difficulties for the writer, which I'll consider below.

In fantasy there is, I think, a different problem: this is historical in nature, and goes to the very heart of what we think of as 'character' at all. Because this is vital, both in terms of fantasy and writing more generally, I'm going to have to digress into the history of how characters have been written into stories over the last thousand years or so. It's a big topic, but stick with me and I'll hope to show you something crucial about your own writing practice.

History of character (I): from type to character

Speaking broadly, there are two major events in the history of 'writing people into stories' over the last millennium. We can peg these two events to two particular writers: first Shakespeare (you've heard of him, of course) and second Goethe (you *should* have heard of him – if you haven't, then rap yourself on the knuckles).

Speaking, again, broadly: before Shakespeare, 'character' was thought of as something fixed and defined. Classical and medieval literature tends to deal in types rather than 'characters' in the modern sense. This in turn reflected the way people thought about 'character' in the real world. Many people believed in a system of 'humours', where the balance between four inner qualities – black bile, yellow bile, phlegm and blood – fixed the sort of person you were: if your black bile predominated you were melancholy; if blood, you were phlegmatic and so on. At the same time, people then believed that the essence of individual was an immortal soul (of course, many people still believe this). Now, a soul is a God-given and indestructible thing; and as such it cannot fundamentally change, for change means augmentation or diminishment and if this latter prevails it would suggest that the immortal substance of a soul was fragile, diminishable and so on. This is not to say that people believed other people were mere automata. Clearly, people can be unpredictable and changeable. The crucial thing for the early modern period was that this 'changeable-ness' was thought of as spiritually determined. God gave you free will, and you could choose to do good or evil. You could (let's say) convert from a life of wickedness to a life of virtue. But that was believed to happen within a more-or-less set, rigid framework.

In practical terms, this meant that characters in stories embodied set types. The hero would be brave, dedicated, strong and noble; the villain would be wicked, devious, mean and so on. In an early 'fantasy' narrative like Spenser's great poem of *The Faerie Queene*, the heroes are good and the villains are bad, and the only challenge in terms of characterization is that the latter are so wicked that they sometime disguise themselves as goodies and must be unmasked. Otherwise all the action takes place within a bright-lit, simplified landscape of fixed subjectivities and ethical certainty.

Many fantasy epics written today take a similarly type-based approach to their characterization. In *The Lord of the Rings*, Aragorn simply *is* noble, brave, determined and heroic. Sauron simply *is* wicked, ruthless, malign and the like.

In the original Old English and medieval texts (which Tolkien knew better than almost anybody), character is something externalized. Nothing goes on 'inside' the heads of these characters; they completely lack the interiority of modern characters. Early in Homer's *Iliad*, Achilles loses his temper with the Achaean king Agamemnon and rushes at him with his sword; but he changes his mind and backs away again – it would, indeed, be a bad idea to kill the king in front of the army! The way Homer writes that Achilles changed his mind is as follows: he has a goddess appear in the air behind the warrior and *catch hold of his hair, pulling him back*. We can take this as a literal appearance, in the magical scheme of the work, or as Homer's externalized metaphor for the thought processes in Achilles' head. Either way, we are dealing with a literary culture that lacks the writerly tools of interiorization.

Once again, we still see this, especially in modes of genre writing that make a virtue of their simplified and pared-down representational logic. Take comic books, or the movies based on them. Instead of writing a character who experiences an intense, inner struggle over whether to do the right thing or to do something self-serving and wicked, these forms of art will often externalize the process. Superman will encounter his evil alter-ego and literally do battle with him. 'Good' Spiderman and 'Wicked' Spiderman will duke it out in the streets of Manhattan. Like the goddess pulling Achilles' hair, we can read this either as a 'reality' within the logic of the story world, or as an externalized metaphor for inner doubts and confusions.

I once interviewed SF legend Brian Aldiss at Cheltenham Literary Festival, and among many other things he talked about how he had never liked *The Lord of the Rings*. Why not? 'Because there are no characters in it – only two-dimensional types.' Straight away he corrected himself: 'No, that's not right. There is one character in the novel, by far the most interesting person in the whole, long book. Gollum. But he's not enough to carry the whole.' Gollum is a 'character' in this sense because, unlike Aragorn, or Sam, or Sauron, he manifests an inner conflict. Elsewhere in the novel when Tolkien wants to dramatize conflict, he externalizes it in terms of the temptation of the ring: Boromir is a noble, heroic warrior-type whose nobleness is 'corrupted' from outside by the ring (on a smaller scale, something similar happens to Frodo). And even with Gollum, who is so completely defined by the influence the ring has on him that his struggles to do the right thing take place within that horizon and start to resemble something like 'modern' characterization – even with him, there is a pull towards externalization. Gollum, for instance, refers to himself in the third person.

'Types' have been sturdy warhorses of genre writing for a long time, and I do not lightly suggest you abandon them. But they are limiting. In *Star Trek*, Captain Kirk, Spock and Bones are 'types': virtuous, heroic, noble, brave – everything an audience can root for. What, then, of those aspects of human personality that are less attractive? Well, in the *Star Trek* universe they are separated out into a whole other cosmos: the 'mirror universe', where versions of Kirk, Spock and Bones who are perfectly evil exist. This is a memorable conceit, and its instincts are right – that perfect goodness is dramatically inert, and that some ethical and individual conflict is necessary. But it's rather crude, too.

This is one of the reasons why Shakespeare is held in such esteem in literary circles – because he revolutionized the way we thought about 'character'. American critic Harold Bloom puts it with characteristic hyperbole when he claims that Shakespeare 'invented the human'; and what he means is that he invented a new way of thinking about and looking at what it means to be human. By writing characters like Hamlet, Lear, Cleopatra, Othello, Macbeth and Lady Macbeth, Shakespeare was doing more than crafting memorable stage icons – he was redefining the way 'character' is thought of. Hamlet acts and is acted upon, but the true interest of the play is not the external action so much as it is the internal drama. To put 'interiority' on stage, Shakespeare adapted an old stage device, the monologue; but nobody before Shakespeare had used monologue like this – to lay bare the processes of subjectivity itself, the way the inwardness of humanity moved and worked. And he combined this with a brilliant sense of how characters interact with one another.

In the old story that Shakespeare adapted, Hamlet is a simple figure: his father, the king, is killed openly in a palace coup; and the usurper threatens to kill Hamlet too, to secure his succession. But Hamlet pretends to be mad, so as to show himself somebody so broken and low that he's beneath notice. The usurper, Claudius, falls for the ruse; and behind his assumed insanity Hamlet plots his revenge. Shakespeare took the bare bones of this story but changed it in crucial ways. In *his* play, the coup is not open – it is believed that the old king simply died. The usurper marries the old king's wife and takes power, but so far from wanting to have young Hamlet killed as a threat to his power, one of the first things he does in the play is adopt Hamlet as his heir. Hamlet need only wait until Claudius dies, and he will be king. He certainly has no need to pretend to be mad in order to save his life. But in Shakespeare's play he pretends to be mad anyway! When we ask ourselves 'why?' we are actually getting to the heart of what makes Shakespeare so great, and revolutionary, a writer of character. Because it's not clear in the play why Hamlet pretends to be mad, or whether his 'pretend' madness shades into actual madness. Hamlet himself does not really know why, because – as Shakespeare was the first to know – our own motivations and inner life are not necessarily open to our rational mind. Freud, centuries later, would build his whole career upon this insight. Character is not clear, reasonable, externalized or fixed; it is, on the contrary, puzzling, moving sometimes in irrational ways, fluid and internal. There are no characters as rich, or resonant, or evocative as these before Shakespeare; there are many afterwards. In this way Shakespeare 'invented the human'. As a writer, you could do worse than create characters as memorable!

History of character (II): from stasis to *Bildungsroman*

Bildungsroman is a German word with many syllables in it, which I like to use because I'm a bit pretentious. A less academic way of saying it is 'character arc'. This is so common, especially in screenwriting, that it's tempting to think it's always been part of the way character has been conceived. But there's a persuasive argument that the very notion of a 'character arc' was invented at the end of the eighteenth century by one man: Johann Wolfgang von Goethe.

 Key idea

Goethe (1749–1839) is surely the most famous German writer there has ever been. He produced major work in a dizzying variety of fields, including some of the greatest poetry ever written in German, dramas that are still performed today, and a wealth of aesthetic, scientific and philosophical criticism. But it is as a novelist that we're mostly concerned with him here.

The idea at the heart of the *Bildungsroman* is that character can change, grow and evolve over time. *Bildung* is etymologically linked to the English 'building' (it means 'education' or 'growth'); and *Roman* means 'novel' – so the term transliterates as 'novel of personal growth' or 'personal education'. But before the eighteenth century, I think for the reasons I mention above, this wasn't how stories were conceived. Achilles is strong, brave, angry and impetuous at the beginning of his story; and he's exactly the same at the end. King Arthur is the same noble king at the end of his 'character arc' as he is at the beginning, whatever external triumphs he has enjoyed or setbacks he has endured.

This is, indeed, so counter-intuitive that it is worth dwelling upon it. Let's stick with the novel. One of the best-selling novels of the eighteenth century was Samuel Richardson's *Pamela* (1740). It is the story of a humble serving maid, the titular Pamela, who is desired by the wicked Lord B. When Pamela virtuously resists the Lord's attempted seduction, he kidnaps her and locks her in his stately home. Then, with the help of his followers, he subjects poor Pamela to all manner of pressure and indignity, up to – but, fortunately for the heroine, not including – actual rape. Throughout this prolonged ordeal, Pamela virtuously resists his advances, until eventually Lord B gives up. Instead of raping Pamela he marries her; she is delighted with this turn of events and revels in the sudden improvement in her social status. The novel closes with this 'happy' ending.

Now the thing that most interests me about Pamela is the way the central figure is characterized. She is a blithe, innocent, beautiful, charming girl at the beginning of the story; and at the end of the story, despite all the truly horrible things that have happened to her, she is exactly the same blithe, innocent, beautiful, charming girl. Readers at the time did not find this improbable; although modern readers, I think, tend to. After all, Pamela is young and open-hearted at the beginning of the novel, and she undergoes a series of horrible assaults, lives for a long time imprisoned against her will and under constant threat of rape. She would surely be (a modern reader thinks) traumatized by her experience.

But thinking like that is precisely to think like a modern. In the eighteenth century and earlier, people thought of 'character' as more fixed than that. People, the perceived wisdom was, don't really change. Even Shakespeare, although he had an extraordinary insight into the inwardness and complexity of human character, didn't tend to show his characters changing over the course of their stories. Cordelia is beautiful and virtuous and loving at the start of *King Lear*; and despite suffering terrible reverses she is precisely as beautiful and virtuous and loving at the end. Iago is wicked as *Othello* opens, and unrepentantly wicked as it closes.

One book changed this: Goethe's *Wilhelm Meister*. Actually, this is two books (*Wilhelm Meisters Lehrjahre*, 1795, and *Wilhelm Meisters Wanderjahre*, 1821) tracing the life of a young gentleman making his way in the world. And over the course of this work he gradually evolves as a person. It seems common sense to us, but it was revolutionary in its day.

Jane Austen, one of the finest novelists ever to have written in English, understood this profoundly. *Emma* (1815) – my favourite among her novels, incidentally – is about a clever, beautiful woman who grows and changes; not because violent or extreme things happen to her, but because (Austen knows) growth and change are the idiom of the human heart. She becomes, slowly, aware of her own selfishness and capacity for small social cruelties and, chastened, grows into a better person.

By the twentieth century this notion of the 'character arc' had become so ubiquitous that a story in which a character did *not* change and evolve became the exception. And there's a danger this could go the other way, and crash into that Hollywood cliché in which every single character has an arc, is on a 'journey', discovers things not only about the world but about themselves. This is not only soppy: it is poorly observed. Sometimes people do change, of course; and sometimes that change can be a profound evolution of personality. But often people do not change; and some stick stubbornly to their old selves in the teeth of the most extraordinary provocations.

What does all this mean for the way you write characters? The crucial thing is to be aware that characters are different to types, and to accept that you will need both for your story.

- Types are a bundle of more or less fixed personality traits, embodied in the way they act, the way they speak, their attitudes and beliefs – and, accordingly, by the way they react. You write types from the outside; and often it is enough simply to describe their exteriority.

- Characters are both externalized (they look and act a certain way in the world) and internalized (they have an inner psychodrama, they are conflicted or evolving or perhaps they are something of a mystery to themselves). Characters are complex and changeable.

The rule of thumb is that the closer an individual is to the heart of the story, the more like a character they need to be. And, conversely, the further away the more like types they may be. This is a purely practical matter: your story will have many minor characters in it: spear-carriers, stormtroopers or redshirts. You will need a main protagonist, but you will also need people to serve them in shops; you need mice who become footmen. If your story is about a brilliant, conflicted scientist whose invention will change the world forever, you probably do want to make her a character interesting in her own right: complex, changeable, conflicted and a little opaque in her motivations even to herself. But if you write every single character in the story that way, it will become a swamp of fluid subjectivity through which the reader will have the most acute trouble navigating. If the story requires your lead scientist to be opposed by Professor Bonehedd of the Traditional Institute of Scientific Conservation, it's fine to make the Professor a two-dimensional rather than a three-dimensional character. He will be in the story only for a few brief appearances. Don't worry about working depth and complexity into him.

Dickens was especially good at this. In David Copperfield and Pip (from *Great Expectations*), he wrote complex, believable and changing characters. But these protagonists are surrounded by a large supporting cast of often grotesque, fixed caricatures – exaggerated in speech and action, monomaniacal or marionettish. And however mannered Dickens's portrayal, he still generates a sense of real life in his writing, because this is how we move through life.

We, at the heart of our own life stories, know how complex and deep and special we are. And there are some people around us – a lover, a best friend, a key family member – whom we think of as possessing a similar depth and complexity. But then there are rings and rings of other people in our lives who exist for us only as Dickensian caricatures. We know intellectually that each of them exists at the heart of their own life stories as rich, strange, complex human beings – but we only have so much time in our day, and so much brain space to devote to them. So we peg them, fix them as types: the co-worker who is a fanatical Arsenal fan, the friend of a friend who married their high-school sweetheart and lives in a semi-detached house in the suburbs. This sort of pigeonholing is socially useful – when we bump into them we can say 'Hi, how's Derek and the kids?' or 'I see the Gunners beat West Ham last night!' and give the impression that we know and care about them. Indeed, if we have pegged people in our lives as types after this fashion, and they change, it can be rather annoying in a small way: 'Oh, Del and I divorced'; 'I have to say, I've rather gone off football – I'm more into morris dancing these days.' We might express sadness at the news of our friend-of-a-friend's divorce, but some part of us is thinking, with mild annoyance, 'You've no business changing the nature of the pigeonhole in which, for my own convenience, I have deposited you!'

 ## Key idea: Mrs Brown

Virginia Woolf invented a notional 'Mrs Brown' as a way of talking about 'the small, downtrodden, eminently common, everyday little person' who, despite her humbleness, expresses something deeply important about what it means to be a human. Ursula Le Guin took this concept and expanded it in a famous essay, 'Science Fiction and Mrs. Brown' (1979). Her point is the extreme rareness with which characters like 'Mrs Brown' appear in science fiction, and the plethora of boring, implausible, two-dimensional, lantern-jawed, heroic space captains.

Depth is an illusion, of course – in a sense, everything is an illusion. There isn't really any 'Hamlet' or any 'Madame Bovary' or any 'Gollum'; there are only words on a page. How you generate that illusion is the crucial question.

The trick is layering.

This is the difference between the way the world sees us and the way we know ourselves to be. Most of us feel that the world doesn't see the real us – we appear more confident at work than we feel, deep down; for many people, this can become a situation where we feel ourselves secretly almost to be frauds. We half expect somebody to blow the whistle – what are *you* doing studying for this university degree? Or holding down this demanding job? Out you go!

So common, indeed, is this state of affairs that a character who *didn't* feel this, to one degree or another, would be either a monster of arrogance or a psychopath. Perfect self-confidence is a very rare and rather alarming human trait. Hannibal Lecter possesses it; your reader does not.

By layering, though, I do not mean 'backstory'. Packing in great wads of backstory behind your character will do nothing but weigh the book down and slow the reader up. Stephen King says one of a great many wise and worthwhile writerly things when he says, 'The most important things to remember about backstory are that (a) everyone has a history and (b) most of it isn't very interesting.' Bring in backstory only as and when it is relevant to the ongoing story, and then do so with a light touch.

Key idea: seven story roles

Russian formalist critic Vladimir Propp broke down thousands of Russian folk tales in his *Morphology of the Folk Tale* (1928) and derived the following list of 'types' (rather than characters) who were deployed to make the story happen.

1 The villain – struggles against the hero.
2 The dispatcher – makes the lack known and sends the hero off.
3 The (usually magical) helper – helps the hero in their quest.
4 The princess or prize and her father – the hero deserves her throughout the story but is unable to marry her because of an unfair evil, usually because of the villain. The hero's journey is often ended when he marries the princess, thereby beating the villain.
5 The donor – gives the hero some helpful, usually magical, object.
6 The hero or victim/seeker hero – reacts to the donor, weds the princess.
7 The false hero – takes credit for the hero's actions or tries to marry the princess.

It is an exercise students of narratology are given in their first year: how well do these categories map on to the story of modern tales like *Star Wars* or *The Lord of the Rings*?

Characterization: using science fiction to your advantage

A mundane writer is limited, in terms of characterization, by the sorts of personalities that actually exist in the world. Now this is not much of a limitation, I have to say: that there is such beautiful variety and profusion of difference of human personality and character is one of the glories of existence. But a writer of science fiction has access to this, and also to a spread of possibilities that the writer of mundane fiction cannot access.

An SF story is predicated upon a novum, a 'new thing'; and while the novum might be an invented piece of technology, a weapon or mode of transport, it could also be – precisely – a kind of personality.

Here are some examples. We know what it is to live inside the subjectivity of a single individual, because we all do it. What might it be to live inside the subjectivity of a hive-mind? Say: a group of clones telepathically linked to one another.

What happens to conventional personality is that some of the human constants are altered. We know what people are like at 20 years of age, or at 70. What might a person be like if they lived to be one thousand? Or one million?

Our personalities are subject to a sine-wave pattern of waking and sleeping, in which the sleeps replenish and re-energize our minds for the day. What if sleep were abolished? As things stand, if a person is sleep-deprived for a certain period they, in effect, go mad and die – but this is science fiction! Let's imagine a future in which the physiological and mental needs of sleep are attended to by certain carefully designed processor implants in the brain tissue. Now worker productivity can be doubled, and nobody need sleep. But what would happen to the regular types of personality in such a situation? How would they alter?

Workshop

Kim Stanley Robinson – one of the single most important writers of science fiction working today – developed an intriguing new twist on the medieval concept of the humours. He adds in two modern conceptions of character that you'll doubtless know – introversion and extraversion. An introvert tends to be more inward, contemplative, perhaps shy and unforthcoming in social situations; an extravert orients his/her life more with respect to outward things, is more at ease in company, and may appear more forceful and energetic. Robinson inflects each of the four medieval character types with these two swerves: the impulsive, aggressive choleric person; the serious and moody melancholic person; the light-hearted and playful sanguine person and the dependable, reasonable and thoughtful phlegmatic person. So four by two gives us eight distinct character types – more than enough for most writerly purposes.

Your exercise is to assign names and roles to each of these eight types:

1 The extravert-choleric individual
2 The introvert-choleric individual
3 The extravert-melancholic individual
4 The introvert- melancholic individual
5 The extravert-sanguine individual
6 The introvert-sanguine individual
7 The extravert-phlegmatic individual
8 The introvert- phlegmatic individual.

This will give you a cast for any ensemble-piece story you may want to tell. How does it fit with your ongoing novel idea?

Summary

This has been a rather more discursive chapter than the others in this volume, in order to lay out the ways in which 'character' has been conceived. It's fine to start with a type (hero and villain, princess and helper), so long as you develop the type at least some of the way in the direction of being an actual character. You do this by (a) giving him/her some psychological motion, the sense that they do or at least could grow and change, and (b) giving him/her some twist or hidden spot in their make-up, something that can't be rationally reduced to a schema. We may be writing science fiction, but, to quote E.M. Forster: 'Science, when applied to personal relationships, is always just wrong.' Character and interpersonal relations are an art, not a science. If they were the latter, Sheldon Cooper would be the most charismatic and well-connected individual in the world.

Where to next?

The next chapter offers a more broadly conceived examination of seven of the most common tropes and conceits of science fiction and fantasy, looking at each one with a view to exploring ways of making every one of them new and fresh. Some of these may be liable to make an appearance in your ongoing novel project.

8

Seven key SF and fantasy tropes

I am only repeating myself when I say that science fiction and fantasy are both fundamentally about breaking out of the pigeonholes of the conventional, the ordinary, the expected and the mundane. This chapter is going to discuss a number of key tropes, or figures, in these genres; not by way of establishing a set of rules you must follow but, on the contrary, by suggesting ways you can reboot the clichés. If you want to write science fiction or fantasy, the chances are you'll want to include one, or maybe more, of the following:

- The alien
- The spaceship
- Psionics
- Time travel
- Wizards and she-zards
- The quest
- The dragon.

The alien

The extraterrestrial; the visitor; the space creature – everything from the devouring blob to a superintelligent shade of the colour blue. Science fiction is, in a radical sense, about the encounter with otherness.

 Pierre Delalande

'The reason I think science fiction is the crucial literature of the 20th century is that it is the only one to put greeting the alien at its heart. And that's important because the 20th century is the one where humanity changed from inward-looking village creatures to creatures forced to encounter otherness on a global scale all the time. How well we manage that encounter, how well we can accept rather than hate and try to kill the other, will define the viability of the human future. There could hardly have been a more important topic! And it is at the heart of SF.'

Writing good extraterrestrial life forms is, as so much else in writing, a balancing act. You are trying to capture the 'otherness'; but if your aliens are too alien then readers will be baffled or bored by them. A reader needs some point of familiarity in order to connect with or care about them; your job is to stretch that familiarity as far as you can without it snapping.

You might make your aliens humanoid (more or less), which will give readers imaginative purchase on them. They could appear human because they have assumed a human-like form (perhaps so as not to startle us too greatly on the first meeting); or they might have humanoid features – two legs, two arms, one head and so on – because they have just evolved that way on their own home worlds. It is so vastly unlikely a thing that evolution (a chain of unnumbered branches of the genetic mutation tree shaped by the purely contingent pressures of local environment) could go from microbe to man in almost the same way on two different sides of the galaxy that most SF writers who follow this model – *Star Trek*, for example – do so with the tacit rationale that humanoid DNA was 'seeded' through the galaxy by some prior alien species.

Star Trek is a key example. Though popular with SF authors on its initial televisualization, some picked holes in the logic of its imagined alien life forms. Vulcans, for instance, evolved on Planet Vulcan, which is a much harsher world than Earth with a markedly higher gravity. In addition to being more logical and less emotional, Vulcans are physically stronger and more resilient than humans, and generally taller and slimmer. As Isaac Asimov noted in the 1960s, a species evolving on a higher gravity world would not be taller and thinner than humans, but shorter and squatter. Whether this matters to you, or would be likely to matter to your readers, is a judgement call.

Putting it like that is by way of saying: 'Nobody really minds the inconsistencies in the world-built aliens of *Star Trek*.' In *Star Trek: The Next Generation* a story was retconned to explain why so many of the aliens looked like human beings with slightly different ears or foreheads – it was because an alien species known only as 'the ancient humanoids' seeded the galaxy with versions of its DNA. (If you're really interested, you'll find this in *Star Trek: The Next Generation*, Series 6 Episode 20, 'The Chase', which was first aired on 26 April 1993.) But this matters less than you might think; because what people love about the different types of alien on *Star Trek* is not how they fit into a consistently thought-through imaginary cosmos, but rather how they speak to human concerns and fascinations. So, the thing so many people love about Vulcans is not the specifics of their body shape, but the way they live strictly rational and logical lives. Vulcans speak to the inner Asperger's individual inside all of us. Klingons are ways of thinking through our belligerence, anger and hostility. In fact, a whole book could be written about how *Star Trek* positions its alien species, and its characters, around this axis: a central mode of being in the world that is part reason and part passion – flanked by an embodiment of pure reason/no passion on one side, and no reason/pure passion on the other. Kirk with Spock and Bones beside him. Picard with Data and Wolf. Humanity between the Vulcans and the Klingons.

This, then, is the secret meaning of aliens in science fiction. It's fine to work through a properly considered thought experiment exploring how life might have evolved under different conditions in other parts of the galaxy – but, in writerly terms, this will remain nothing more than an intellectual exercise unless the resulting aliens connect in some symbolic or expressive way with the human emotions of your reader.

Terrifying aliens like Hans Geiger's acid-for-blood creature, or H.G. Wells's Martians, speak to our fears and our repulsions. Repulsion is a strangely powerful force in the human psyche – if repulsive things merely repelled us it would be a simple matter; but, oddly, repulsive things are at once repellent and weirdly compelling.

Invading aliens (which may or may not be like these terrifying alien monsters) speak to a more specifically paranoid sense of our fear and repulsion.

Logical, rational, superior aliens speak to our complex relationship with our own rational, logical sides. This, again, is a conflicted matter – it is, of course, good to be intelligent and rational; but to be super-intelligent, preternaturally logical and rational (like Sherlock Holmes) is both admirable and alarming – because there is something pitiless and inhuman about too perfect an intellectual capacity.

Cuddly, friendly, cute aliens are feelgood, and might be about our relationship to pets, or kids. If you're going to write a story like Spielberg's *E.T.*, you need to work out why the cutesy alien needs to be an alien at all – why not make it a talking puppy, or a magical foundling.

Sexy aliens are not unknown in science fiction – David Bowie's 1970s career both as pop star and as the lead actor in Nicholas Roeg's *The Man Who Fell to Earth* (1976) was based around the idea of, to quote the man himself, 'loving the alien'. And our feelings of sexual attraction and desire, especially if those feelings don't fit into the conventional forms our society dictates, can usefully find expression via this type. But it is worth noting that, over the last decade or so, the key vehicle for the fictional articulation of this particular mode of emotional intensity has not been science-fictional, but rather a figure from the repertoire of horror and fantasy – the vampire.

Write about an alien

Invent an alien. Simple as that. In 500–750 words, write an
account of an alien life form. Identify what the alien-ness of your
alien connotes, and find a way of showing (not telling) that.

The spaceship

For many SF writers, spaceships are nothing more than glorified
cars, planes or boats. Of course, they are *identified* as spaceships:
they are described as being bigger, warp-powered, hideously
beweaponed and so on; and they are set in play for whatever story
the writer or film-maker is telling – but there is no attention to the
actual practicalities of flying through space. *Battlestar Galactica* is,
in essence, a US Navy aircraft carrier – in space. The USS *Enterprise*
is a US Navy destroyer – in space. They have crews similar in size
(why? Wouldn't future automatic technologies, advance fly-by-wire
and computing render almost all the crew jobs on the *Enterprise*
redundant?); they are structured with decks and corridors and
rooms, just like a naval ship (such structural constraints make sense
in Earth's gravity, but are hardly how one would design a starship
from scratch).

Star Wars contains all three things. It should not surprise us that
George Lucas's first, Oscar-winning and breakout movie (1973's
American Graffiti) is, among other things, a homage to the
liberating potential of the automobile for small-town American
teen life. The *Star Wars* universe treats its smaller spacecraft in just
this way – as car- or truck-sized machines for getting about in. Its
X-wing fighters fly like World War II aircraft, and its Imperial
battleships are like large naval vessels.

The advantage of this is audience familiarity: we know how actual
naval vessels operate, and we can relate to spaceships conceived
along similar lines (and SF tradition has rendered this manner
of spaceship design so familiar it's become a lazy shorthand
for unimaginative writers – a cliché, in other words). But the

disadvantages are more pressing. The main problem is one we've mentioned before: science fiction as mere fancy dress – if you want to write a story about cowboys and Indians, write it; don't call the cowboys 'space frontiersmen' and the Indians 'four-armed Skrks' and set the story on a thinly realized Mars. Similarly, if you want to write about the US Navy, you should write about the US Navy. There are many exciting stories to be told about that body of dedicated serving men and women. They don't need to be gussied-up with space lapels and sent to Alpha Dollarturai.

A connected problem is one of over-familiarity: science fiction affords you almost unlimited imaginative possibilities; why hobble your story by wheeling out the creaky, cobwebbed props and settings of a thousand prior stories? Make it new!

In the case of spaceships, this means doing more than simply translating something you're familiar with, adding a few extra turrets and laser cannons and calling it a spaceship. It means thinking through what a spaceship is, from the ground up.

On Earth, vessels like destroyers have to be rigid structures in order to function. Their outer dimensions are determined by the exigencies of the ocean and their inner layout by the compromise between human needs and limited space. But in space none of these things would apply.

One shortcut to the sense-of-wonder so often prized in science fiction is the very enormous super-massive space-dreadnought! Nothing wrong with that, except that there is no actual material that could maintain rigidity on the scale of (say) a Borg cube, or the *Star Wars* universe's 'Super Star destroyers'. If such colossal structures didn't merely break apart when thrust was applied, they would at least bulge and distort like vast balloons as they moved. So, turn this around: if it's important to you to write about an absolutely huge starship, why not conceive of it as structurally more like a jellyfish than a rigid structure?

FASTER THAN LIGHT (FTL)

Nothing with mass can travel faster than light. This is not an arbitrary speed limit imposed by some notional physics authority; it is a fundamental aspect of the geometry of the universe. Saying 'the spaceships travels faster than light' is not like saying 'the aircraft travels faster than sound'; it is instead like saying 'the triangle has four sides'. The vast majority of science fiction ignores this fundamental rule of physics because the distances between the stars are so immense that travel between them at sub-light speeds would take decades, centuries or millennia. Nonetheless, this is what science says.

Focus point

How would *Star Wars* work if the only travel possible happened at sub-light speeds? It would lose its instantaneity, its kinetic rushing around and immediate adventuring – but would that necessarily be a bad thing? Luke Skywalker might travel for decades (perhaps in suspended animation) to fight Darth Vader, only to discover that his adversary had died of old age in the interim. How would the 'space opera' universe be altered under these sorts of constraints?

Science fiction has developed a number of cheats to get around the problem. Two – hyperspace or wormholes – have some basis in physics, although it is currently thought that the amount of energy required to open a wormhole would be impracticably vast – it might take the whole mass of the Sun converted into energy to open a small wormhole from here to the nearest star. Under what circumstances would that be a price worth paying? (That's a serious question: is there a story idea there?)

Hyperspace depends on the notion that there are other dimensions apart from the four we inhabit (length, breadth, height, time), and that travel through them might get us to the stars more quickly. But what if hyperspatial dimensions were accessed and found to be much longer than our physical ones? How might these 'long cuts' be used in your story?

ANTI-GRAVITY

In H.G. Wells's novel *The First Men in the Moon*, a scientist named Cavour invents an anti-gravity substance which, modestly, he calls Cavorite. He builds a spaceship out of this and uses it to travel to the moon. Anti-gravity has been a staple of science fiction ever since. However, anti-gravity violates physics.

Wells's mistake was in thinking that gravity applies a force to the body in the way a strong wind applies a force; and that it could therefore be blocked by a sort of 'wind-break' or shield. We now know that gravity is not some external flow or pressure, but rather the curvature of spacetime, part of the geometry of the cosmos. To create 'anti-gravity' would mean manipulating spacetime itself and, if we could do *that*, then making anti-grav boots would be the least of our ambitions. More, what post-Einstein scientists call 'the equivalency principle' means that any anti-gravity device would also be an anti-inertia device. Inertia is the resistance of a body to acceleration. What might physics look like if we no longer had to apply a force to get a mass to accelerate – if Newton's F=ma no longer applied?

James Blish's *Cities in Flight* series of novels is based on the idea of a 'spindizzy', a machine that generates anti-gravity. The twist is that this machine is more efficient the more mass it is applied to, such that it is easier to lift the whole city of New York than a single spaceship. The series is, deservedly, a classic of science fiction; but how might the story go in a universe where F=ma were no longer a valid equation of physics?

ARTIFICIAL GRAVITY

And again: gravity is not something that can be created out of nothing (it's not, in other words, like the wind that can be imitated just by turning on a big fan). The only way to create actual gravity is by bending spacetime, and the only way we know to do *that* is by accumulating a very large amount of mass. 'Artificial gravity' has become a staple of, especially, TV and cinematic science fiction, where it is simply easier to film, as well as more identifiable for the audience, to have your space marines and boldly-goers walking around the corridors and hangars of the spaceship as if it were on Earth. To provide astronauts with the experience of walking around as if on Earth, you would need a spaceship with the mass of Earth. It need not be the *size* of Earth – it might be much denser, or built around an Earth-mass singularity; but it would require excessive amounts of energy to move it!

The only way we know of mimicking gravity is acceleration. It would be possible to accelerate a spaceship such that the crew were pushed back with a force equivalent to gravity (Alastair Reynolds's *Revelation Space* novels include 'lighthugger' spaceships that do this). This would require some form of thrust not presently achievable (it is well beyond what we can do with our current chemical rockets, for instance) but *is* possible within the laws of physics. From the point of view of the people left behind, a ship accelerating so as to create the effect of 0.5g – the crew would feel one half as heavy as they do on Earth – would appear to get near to the speed of light after about a year, during which time it would have travelled about half a light year. It could then keep accelerating for as long as it had power to do so: from the point of view of those left behind it would get closer and closer to the speed of light on a hyperbola without ever reaching it, and would take however many years to travel to its destination as its destination was light years distant. From the point of view of the people on board the ship, the acceleration would simply continue, and the time dilation effects predicted by Einstein would mean that for them much less time would appear to pass than for an external observer.

As a rule of thumb, for a constant acceleration at one (Earth) G, the ship journey time will be the distance in light years to the destination, plus one year. This rule of thumb will give answers that are slightly shorter than the exact calculated answer, but reasonably accurate.

Psionics

Telepathy, or psionics, is one of those things that doesn't exist. The mind is not built like a radio transmitter/receiver. The good news is that we don't need telepathy. I can 'read' your mind, and you can 'read' mine via the simple expedient of a little thing humans have evolved called 'talking to one another'. If we're too far apart to do this face to face, we can utilize things like 'phones'. If you want to know what I'm thinking, I can tell you. And vice versa.

Putting it like this, of course, pinpoints the fictional appeal of telepathy – that is to say, its symbolic appeal. We can boil this down to two things. One is the question as to whether you can trust me to tell you how I'm really feeling. I might lie. How can you be sure how I'm feeling? Accordingly, it would useful for (say) an officer of the law – like Judge Dredd's colleague Judge Anderson – to be able to read minds. The flipside here has to do with the invasion of privacy.

We have elaborate laws to restrict the access law enforcement is permitted to our private lives, and for good reason. What if, instead of our fictional telepath being a benign authority figure like the *X-Men*'s Professor Xavier, s/he was a wicked person? Imagine a police state in which Big Brother did more than simply watch you through a telescreen, but was able literally to read your mind 24/7. What sort of story could you tell about such a place?

Two, I think, is the question of intimacy. Words and physical hugging get us close to the objects of our desire; but telepathy would get us closer still. This is the sort of dream some might find claustrophobic, but others – especially people who feel more acutely alienated from human contact than normal – might yearn for. How would Romeo and Juliet have played out if the two lovers were telepathically linked to one another?

 Michio Kaku

'In science fiction, telepaths often communicate across language barriers, since thoughts are considered to be universal. However, this might not be true. Emotions and feelings may well be nonverbal and universal, so that one could telepathically send them to anyone, but rational thinking is so closely tied to language that it is very unlikely that complex thoughts could be sent across language barriers. Words will still be sent telepathically in their original language.'

There is a third mode of imaginative entry into the world of the telepath – the notion that having telepathic powers would enable you to compel others to do your bidding. I have to say I don't much like this: as a power-over fantasy it is deplorable, and as a science-fiction conceit it is unnecessary ... after all, evil people have been compelling others to do their bidding using only words for thousands of years. But if it appeals to you, I'd say it will tend to unpack into two kinds of story. Either – as in John Wyndham's masterly *The Midwich Cuckoos* (1957) – wicked others (aliens, Nazis, stockbrokers, whatever) are using their powers to control the masses, and the story will hinge upon how and with what cost their power can be thwarted. Or – and it's harder to think of stories that do this – 'good' people hope to use their powers to bring about a utopia, in which case the story will probably be one of unintended consequences, moral rot, power corrupting and so on.

Think through your telepathy conceit. Is it a latent natural power? (In which case, what brings it to maturity?) Or is it a technological prosthesis or medium that enables it?

Does it cost your protagonist anything to 'do' telepathy? Does it, for instance, involve a concomitant wasting away of the body? Does it put him/her at risk from hostile 'normals'?

Is your telepathy a link between two people, or a mode by which one person can read the minds of many or perhaps all other people? If the latter, how does s/he filter their 'gift'? Maybe they can't, and it has driven them mad.

In a world in which everybody was a telepath, the rare individual who was telepathically inert might become the superhero. For everybody else, the weird opacity of this individual's mind, the impossibility of being able to read them, might give them special powers.

Time travel

The history of travelling in time is a curious one. It was, to all intents and purposes, invented out of whole cloth by one man – H.G. Wells (him again) – remarkably late in the day, with the short novel *The Time Machine* (1895). This is where 'time travel' itself starts as a fictional form. We might wonder how it is that time travel came from nowhere in 1894 to become one of the most popular modes of fantastical and science-fictional storytelling of the twentieth and twenty-first centuries. To be clear, it is the standing-start nature of this runaway success that is most intriguing. For a generation now, time travel has been something like a cultural dominant. TV has seen the extraordinary popularity of the BBC series *Doctor Who* (1963–present). *Star Trek* (first broadcast in 1966), a show that stands with *Doctor Who* in the 'most globally influential SF TV series' stakes, very often included time-travel stories in its narrative; and many of its spin-off movies involved time travel, from *Star Trek IV: The Journey Home* (1986) to the rebooted J.J. Abrams *Star Trek* (2009). Contemporary box-office successes include many such texts, from *The Time Traveller's Wife* (2009) to the *Harry Potter* movies (which include a 'time turner' among their magical props). At the end of the first *Superman* movie (1978), the hero undoes Lex Luthor's villainy and resurrects his dead girlfriend by turning back time. Latterly, superhero movies out of the Marvel or DC franchise have come to dominate global box office, and the most recent of these, *X-Men: Days of Future Past* (2014), is a time-travel drama.

I'm not suggesting that there were absolutely no time-travel stories before Wells. A few years earlier, Edward Page Mitchell published 'The Clock that Went Backward' (1881) about a magic grandfather clock that enables characters to go back to the siege of Leyden in 1572 and save the city. In Dickens's *A Christmas Carol* (1844), magic spirits gift Scrooge glimpses of his past and future. But immediately we can see a difference – these are both magical fantasies, not quasi-scientific extrapolations; and they did not spawn successors in the way that Wells's story did.

Time travel is evidently a trope that scratches a very widespread cultural itch. Given that fact, it is strange that nobody before Wells had thought of it. It can hardly be that the 1890s saw the birth of a radically new kind of person, interested in the implications of time travel in a way not true of people in the 1870s.

The true significance of Wells's *Time Machine*, in other words, is not its narrative motion but its mechanism – its device, its in-story vehicle. We're not primarily interested in the time traveller; we're interested in his car. As Marty McFly put it so memorably, his voice freighted equally with wonder and material envy: 'You built a time machine *out of a DeLorean*?' For *Doctor Who* fans the *TARDIS* is as much a character as any of the doctor's interchangeable assistants.

Time travel has been dominated by a kind of machine-ness. But this 'mechanism' has disadvantages as well as advantages. One is that time travel as a subgenre has come to be dominated by a series of clockwork-like 'paradoxes', working themselves out.

There are two of these that are particularly famous: the so-called 'grandfather paradox' and a looser class of 'time loop' paradoxes. These can be pleasing, formally and even aesthetically; but before we look at them it's worth noting that there's another less machinic aspect to 'time travel', neither magical nor yet machinic. We call this 'memory' (and its shadow, 'anticipating'). Marcel Proust's

A la recherche du temps perdu (1913–27) is rarely categorized as science fiction but it is in fact a huge, complex and powerful meditation on the way our minds travel in time all the time. It is entirely uninterested in the spurious neatness of mechanical paradoxes and loops.

GRANDFATHER PARADOXES

Assume time travel is possible. What would happen if I went back in time and killed my grandfather? He would die, so I would never be born, so I wouldn't exist and wouldn't be able to travel back, so my grandfather *wouldn't* die, so I *would* be born, so I would be able to travel back, so my grandfather would die, so I would never be born, so I wouldn't exist and wouldn't be able to travel back, so my grandfather *wouldn't* die, so … you get the picture.

There are several 'solutions' offered to address this paradox, by philosophers as well as SF writers (the latter generally come up with more interesting solutions …) and all, except maybe the first, entail rich possibilities for storytelling.

1 The grandfather paradox proves that time travel is impossible.

2 The form of the paradox resembles a feedback loop. Now we know what happens with real-life runaway feedback, for instance when a circuit shorts out or when a microphone picks up and amplifies the hum from its speaker. In other words, what would happen if you were ever able to go back in time and kill your grandfather would be a BANG! and the whiff of temporal scorching, as you, grandfather, and a bunch of related things exploded out of time. How this would leave the remaining timeline is up for debate. Maybe unexplained explosions like the 1908 Tunguska event was not a meteorite impact at all, but the result of something like this?

3 The most popular theory about this paradox is that of alternative timelines. The idea is: if you killed your grandfather in 1960, you would change history from that point on; and were you to return to your present you'd arrive in a world subtly, or perhaps hugely, different from the one you remembered. It may be that alternative timelines branch out at every moment of choice, not just from the decisions to commit capital crimes. An influential and much-parodied version of this is Ray Bradbury's

'A Sound of Thunder' (1952), where a time-travelling big-game hunter travelling back to a licensed Tyrannosaurus Rex hunt accidentally steps on a butterfly, such that when he returns to his own time he finds everything different. This styles 'time' as a fragile thing, and many SF writers have imagined a notional 'time police', tasked precisely with preventing 'temporal paradoxes', which has become an SF staple. Isaac Asimov's *The End of Eternity* (1955) concerns a cast of time policemen called 'the Eternals' who travel the timeways keeping humanity from larger harm. In John Brunner's *Times without Number* (1962), the time police are working to preserve a rather oppressive timeline (one in which the Spanish Armada conquered England) that is not our own. In Keith Laumer's *Dinosaur Beach* (1971), different branches of time police are effectively at war with one another, resulting in an extraordinarily intricately plotted story of competing timelines. Terry Pratchett's *Discworld* novels feature the 'History Monks', who manipulate time and history with benevolent intentions.

4 It could be that there is a degree of inertia in time travel that makes it impossible to alter the past – you might go back with the intention of murdering your grandparent only to find that events conspire to make it impossible. Would this be 'providence', or even 'God'? Or would it be something akin to the physical inertia, or the impossibility, of travelling faster than light? In fact, this idea is somewhat the reverse of the time police idea, and, if pursued with enough intellectual rigour, leads to some unsettling conclusions about free will and, despite appearances, our lack of it.

5 This is where you get to think through other possibilities. Maybe, since our memory is both fragile and conditioned to operate according to the lines of force of time's arrow as we generally experience it, travelling back in time would result in profound amnesia (such that we wouldn't be able to remember that we wanted to kill our grandfather). Perhaps, arriving back in the past, you discover that your body doesn't quite 'gel' with the temporal context and you appear more like a ghost than a person. Could you spook your grandfather to death? (We could extend this: maybe ghosts are not the departed spirits of the dead but time travellers from the future desperate to warn us of … what?)

TIME LOOPS

The defining texts as far as this paradox is concerned are two of Robert Heinlein's short stories: 'By His Bootstraps' (1941) and ' – All You Zombies – ' (1958). In the latter the contortions of a temporally dislocated plot result in the main character impregnating a sex-change earlier version of himself who thus gives birth to himself. That there is (it seems to me) something claustrophobic and even psychopathological about this fantasy hasn't stopped it becoming a staple of the genre. Cinema has been particularly taken with the structural neatness of this loopy trope: *Groundhog Day* (1993), *Donnie Darko* (2001), *Déjà Vu* (2006), *Source Code* (2011) and the aptly named *Looper* (2012) all rehearse this structure. Perhaps the most extreme iteration of this kind of story is A.E. van Vogt's *The Weapon Shops of Isher* (1951), in which a time traveller loses control of his craft and ends up shuttling back and forth across huge stretches of time, building up a form of temporal-friction energy the whole while, before ultimately shooting back to the dawn of time and exploding as the Big Bang that creates the cosmos.

The key cinematic texts, though, tend to work through the 'loop' and 'paradox' conceits of science fiction's written texts. Chris Marker's *La Jetée* (1963) starts after a devastating World War III. A prisoner (Davos Hanich) is sent decades back in time to pre-war Paris, where he uncovers the truth behind a memory he has been obsessively rehearsing from his own childhood – standing with a woman (Hélène Chatelain) on the observation pier or 'jetty' of Orly Airport and seeing a man die. The film is composed almost wholly out of black and white still images, a mode that resists the 'temporal' fluidity of conventional cinema and also invokes the memorious habit of consulting still photos of one's own past – because this is a film about childhood memory and trauma working itself out, on a global scale, in adulthood. The key to the memory (the dying man the child saw is that same child as a time-travelling adult) is a surprisingly resonant semiotic knot. Terry Gilliam lost some of this intensity of focus in his remake *12 Monkeys* (1995), although he made up for it with the richness and strangeness of his visual imagination.

Schwarzenegger in *The Terminator* (1984) plays the future-built humanoid robot of the movie's title, sent back in time by a malign, intelligent computer system to kill a woman called Sarah Connor who, in 1980s LA, will give birth to the child John Connor who will grow up to defeat the computer system in its global war against humankind. Future humanity sends one of their own to protect Sarah Connor, and the movie strings together a series of exciting set pieces in which this future-human fights the Schwarzenegger future-robot. The twist is that the future-human and Sarah Connor fall in love; he is John Connor's by-his-bootstraps father and, by attempting to snuff out the threat of Sarah Connor, the wicked 'Skynet' computer system is actually guaranteeing the birth of the very man it was trying to prevent. As with *La Jetée*, the narrative loop has a pleasing symmetry to it, and it flatters our (human) sensibilities to think that 'chronology', however it is messed about with, will shake down into a timeline in which human beings win.

Another version of the 'loop' conceit is the 'Groundhog Day' iteration of non-progressing time. What would it be like to be trapped in the same day – or hour – or second – for ever? What if, when you die, you are immediately transported back to the moment of your birth, only this time with your adult consciousness and memories? What if this happened every time you died, so that after a thousand lifetimes you acquired a thousand-fold density of consciousness and memory – until you eventually reached escape velocity?

 Charles Yu, *How to Live Safely in a Science Fictional Universe*

'This is what I say: I've got good news and bad news. The good news is, you don't have to worry, you can't change the past. The bad news is, you don't have to worry, no matter how hard you try, you can't change the past. The universe just doesn't put up with that. We aren't important enough. No one is. Even in our own lives. We're not strong enough, wilful enough, skilled enough in chronodiegetic manipulation to be able to just accidentally change the entire course of anything, even ourselves.'

Time travel is so overworked a conceit that it can be hard to think of a way of making it new. Here are some ideas.

What if the only way to travel back in time was one hour per hour, but backwards? In order for a 20-year-old to travel back to a point

20 years before his/her birth s/he would have to live through 40 years of his/her own ageing, and arrive at the temporal destination as a 60-year-old. Who would be prepared to undertake such a trip? What might make it worth while?

One of the arguments sometimes advanced for the impossibility of time travel is 'If anybody were ever to invent it, then we'd know about it, because visitors would have come to us from the future.' But perhaps we're all currently living in the temporal equivalent of a wildlife preserve, an artificially maintained bubble built around us to create a sort of zoo-diversity in an otherwise wholly homogenized timescape. Imagine a character escaping from the 'temporal zoo'. What would she discover? What would a world be like in which travelling in time was as easy as travelling in space is for us?

I'll tell you what I think. Time travel would erase the distinction between past, present and future, just as the advances in global travel have erased distance and cultural specificity. It would result in a kind of temporal globalization: the commodification of the hours and minutes, the homogeneity of memory, hope and perception. Everybody would use the time machines of course; they would employ them for work and for leisure, to the extent that people could no longer imagine what life would be like without them (and, forcefully, they could not be uninvented); and at the same time people would feel elegiac twinges that life was somehow better before they came along.

Wizards and she-zards

Nobody calls a female 'wizard' a 'she-zard', of course. That would be silliness. But its silliness is, actually, my point. Few features of fantasy are as steeped in unquestioned sexism as that of 'the wizard'. The male wizard is wise, profound, skilled, a helper and mentor, of whom the worst we can say is that he's sometimes a little cranky. A she-zard is an enchantress – seductive and dangerous, untrustworthy and wicked, most likely a 300-year-old woman keeping her appearance unnaturally young and beautiful with dangerous dark magic (but who will be revealed as the shrivelled and disgusting old crone she truly is by the end of the story). See? Sexism.

Sir James Frazer, *The Golden Bough*

'There are strong grounds for thinking that, in the evolution of thought, magic has preceded religion.'

With wizards we are dealing with a cultural cliché so deeply embedded that your main task – should you wish to write a wizard – will be in finding a way past the huge briar patch it represents. Everybody knows what a wizard looks like. He looks like Merlin, Gandalf, Dumbledore and the two guitarists from ZZ Top (the latter two are not, so far as I am aware, actual wizards). They are old men with an innate talent for magic who may use a prop – a staff, a wand, a guitar (sorry: that slipped through – as I said before, ZZ Top are not actually wizards) – to focus his magic. He is usually wise, a guider and helper, even if sometimes a rather grumpy one. A mentor to the hero. These wizards also had their evil counterparts – sorcerers, sometimes as yang to the wizardly yin within the same story (as Saruman to Gandalf).

So deeply embedded in the popular consciousness is this archetype that if you write a 'wizard' and specify nothing further about the character, your reader will tend to think of such a blue-cloaked, white-bearded old man. What this means is that, writing your mage, you need to work that much harder to undo the negative power of the cliché. Think again. There are good reasons – beyond the need to wage war on cliché – to reconfigure this archetype for the twenty-first century: do you really want to write a story that tacitly reproduces the idea that wisdom is the exclusive preserve of old white dudes? But you need to be careful, too: simple flip-abouts have their problems.

Take his whiteness. You could make your wizard a person of colour – and perhaps base your magic system on African, Voodoo or the Chinese 'Wu Xia' system. Adding ethnic diversity to the hideous whiteness of too much contemporary fantasy can only be a good thing. But you need to be careful that you're not simply migrating to a different sort of racism. Implying that wisdom and magic is the preserve of bearded elderly white men is obviously problematic; but thinking that there is something 'magical' about black people,

Write about magic

The Old English for 'magic' was *drycræft* (from, the scholars say, the Irish *draidecht*, from which the Romans derived the word 'druid'). I like the idea of magic as drycraft very much; or at least I prefer it to the messier, less precise fluid-spilling wetcræft. Think about the medium of your character's magic – I mean, the way it actually manifests. Be honest with yourself: are you thinking of a kind of cinematic electricity? Rivers of neon blue quote energy unquote pouring out of a staff or a wand? Think again. Imagine a magic that manifested aurally rather than visually; or a magic that operated only smell or taste. The more abstruse the better – because you will be removing the operation of your magic from the too-easy and overconventionalized.

Your task here is to sketch three different magic systems that operate in ways you have never before read about or seen onscreen, and yet which feel somehow right. Aim for intimacy, for some bodily cost in the spell-making and for rules. I'll give you an example.

In the magic discipline of Occja, a mage of either gender can perform spells that affect other people: giving them powers, or afflicting them with illness, making them sleep for decades or turning them into puppets. But the magic is exacting, and difficult. A single hair must be obtained from the person you wish to place under an enchantment. The wizard must take this hair and insert it into the tear duct of his/her left eye (for malign spells) or right (for spells empowering the subject). The longer the hair, and the further up the tear duct the mage is able to insert it, the more powerful the spell. As the insertion is being accomplished the mage must recite the 13-word Charm of Wyseeing. If s/he uses a mirror to aid the task, it must be a mirror of polished bronze – not any other substance. The fresher the hair, the better. When the hair is inserted the mage must look at the subject with the relevant eye (closing the other) and call up the Potency, and then speak the spell.

Your turn:

1

2

3

because you consider them exotic and primitive and closer to the animism of the cosmos, is much more racist. There's a shorthand for this: 'the magical negro'.

The magical negro is a type of character especially frequent in American books and films. S/he is an individual with magical insight, special powers or magical abilities which s/he uses to help the main, white, character. The word 'negro' is used deliberately in this context: it is of course archaic, and considered offensive in modern English (especially in its abbreviated form). The point of referring to such characters is to make plain the extent to which a subordinate magical black character whose purpose is selflessly to help white people is a throwback to stereotypes such as Little Black Sambo and the Noble Savage. My advice: don't write 'magical negro' characters.

Of course your mage can be black, or any other ethnicity. Just make sure that he is not the only person of colour in an otherwise default white world.

Gender is similarly problematic. Folklore and legend speak often of female wizards: they are called 'witches' and are evil. 'Sorceress' is not a neutral feminine version of the word 'wizard'; it is the word wizard translated into Sexistspeak. Sorceresses are seductive, erotic, untrustworthy, ruthless and black-hearted individuals who use their magic only for evil and personal gain.

Story idea

The ancient Egyptians believed there were seven substances produced by the body, and that all seven were needful for proper magic: wax; tears; spit; phlegm; sweat; semen; urine. Faeces and vomit don't count, for reasons that are beyond me. How about a story based on the seven exhalations? (Breath from the nose; breath from the mouth; yawns; odour; burps; wind; spirit – this last being telepathy.)

One feature shared by all fantasy (or other) narratives predicated upon 'magic' is that the magic 'has rules'. This is because magical thinking 'has rules' – psychological rules that is, which have exactly the same coherency and validity as, say, the 'rule' that 'when turning on or off the light, I must flick the switch seven times or my family will die'. Just because the rule is inside a person's head rather than in the world at large doesn't make it less powerful – rather the reverse, indeed.

I'd like to write a fantasy novel in which the magic has no rules at all. How would such a world work? A place of anarchic magic, powers that come on without warning, gifting random individuals with unpredictable powers for an unpredictable length of time. Leading your army into battle, you might find that your lowliest spear carrier was suddenly more powerful than your imperial wizards. In such a world almost all the certainties of generic fantasy would be upended, and a topsy-turvy cosmos of radical uncertainty and instability installed. It probably wouldn't work – which is to say, it probably wouldn't win over a large group of fans, however well I wrote it. My suspicion, formed from reading hundreds and hundreds of these kinds of novels over my life, is that the genre articulates this buried truth: that the millions who think they love fantasy because of the magic actually love it *because of the rules*.

Boris Arachna

'We talk about "real magic" to distinguish it from "stage magic", which, as illusion, is actually not magic at all: a "false magic". But the irony here is that real magic is the kind of magic that can't actually be done; where the "unreal" stage magic is the kind that can really be performed. This is a nice irony, but it's more than that. It's symptomatic of the way performance – under which rubric we might include stage, screen, book, song – upends the logic of actuality.'

The quest

The clichéd 'quest' is another aspect of fantasy writing so deeply embedded in the discourse that it takes some serious imaginative spadework to extricate oneself from it. You know how it goes: a plucky group of unlikely and varied characters band together, pack up their rucksacks, don their cloaks, take their staffs in their right hands and stride out across the land. They must walk – walk, mark you! – all the way from the safe lands of Top Left Bit of Map, through fields and over hills, under mountains and across bogs, down rivers and through enchanted forests (all of which are marked on the map at the start of the book) until they reach the Kingdom of Peril, in the Bottom Right Bit of Map, where they can wrest the Magic Mark of Guffin from the mailed fist of the Lord of Wrongness. Without this magical Mark, the fields of Top Left Bit of Map will no longer be fruitful, the ice will swallow the villages and apocalypse will descend.

There are, as ever, reasons why the quest is so ubiquitous in fantasy. It is extremely useful. It gives you a simple, readily comprehensible overarching structure for your tale, one flexible enough to permit the insertion of any number of incidental episodes and adventures, yet strong enough structurally to give even a thousand pages of printed book some kind of meaningful shape. You can have mini-climaxes at points one-third and two-thirds of the way through – grappling with the fiery Bald-Rog under the chasm of Chrômdôm in Chapter 33, the Battle of the Secondary Sorcerer and his Savage Slave Army in Chapter 66 – and leave room for a world-saving or world-damning (the first, obviously) Grand Battle at the end. And it means that, having carefully sketched out a detailed map, drawing the mountain chains like this – Λ Λ Λ Λ Λ Λ Λ – and the forests with lots of little cotton-bud shaped trees, you won't have wasted your time. Your characters can go on a Cook's Tour of the entire landscape, and you can fill up hundreds of pages with descriptions of the Wharves of the Sea-Dwarves and the Liquid Silver Wells of the Silvan Elves.

But its utility has led to it being chronically over-used, like antibiotics; and a new generation of Super Fan has arisen impervious to its charms. 'Not another bloody quest,' they will sigh, and they will put the book down and go look for something less hackneyed.

Subverting this cliché is going to take work. It won't be enough to (for instance) start at the bottom right of the map and work your way to the top left. It won't be enough to have Samurai instead of elves and jockeys instead of dwarves.

And, actually, this is one cliché that has come down to us through its most influential form already (as it were) pre-upended. The quest in *The Lord of the Rings* is not, as most of the quests in the fantasy tradition had been before Tolkien, for the Holy Grail or the dragon's hoard. That is, it is not a quest to find something. In

The Lord of the Rings, the Fellowship have the something at the beginning; and their quest is to get rid of it – the twist being that there's only one place in Middle Earth (a place which happens to be at the bottom right of the map, where our heroes start top left) where this disposal will be effective.

Your mission, then, is to find ways to make the quest structure fresh and exciting.

Focus point

What other reasons do people have for undertaking long treks?

Why are you thinking of a small band heading off with one specific aim? Why not a large group – or a whole nation? Why a quest – why not a crusade? A trail of tears? A seasonal migration? Why not tourism?

Your fantasyland is a place with magic in it, yes? Then you could have the landscape afflicted with magic, such that a simple journey to the next village (for the heroine to reach her beau on their wedding day, say) becomes an epic trek across the outer reaches of the Land.

What if the trek is only 20 miles, but a magical 'Zeno' curse means that space dilates the further you travel – the first mile takes you half an hour; the next an hour, the next two hours and so on?

Set the object of the quest in an impossible place – impossible, that is, for a medieval individual: on the moon, say. At the bottom of the deepest trench in the Westron Ocean. How are your characters going to achieve this?

The dragon

Dragon, here, is a placeholder term for any of the myriad beasts of fantasy – griffins, trolls, giant snakes, giant arachnids, kaiju, moon-moths, werewolves and badgermans, Frankenstein-monsters, harpies, sirens and balrogs. Anything bigger than a person and liable to scare a person. But rather than embark on an encyclopaedic discussion of all these things, I am going to concentrate on the draconic type. Dragons have a special place in fantasy lore – and by lore I mean 'that reservoir of unimaginative conventions and stock tropes'. We can go further, and look to a collected group of similar fantasy creatures – the big beasts. Ogres twice the size of a man; giant anacondas; Godzillae; dinosaurs – and of course, dragons.

These creatures have, rather obviously, to do with size; and for that reason with scariness. We need to be clear about this, because a lot of feeble fantasy writing proceeds from the idea that it's possible to access the sublime without encountering terror.

 Focus point

Why are fantasy and science fiction so addicted to the very big? Both the SF 'sense of wonder' and the thrilling sense of eldritch transport in fantasy tap our imaginative responses to the sublime – something equally awe-inspiring and terrifying. The cause of this, I think, goes back to childhood. Fantasy, especially, can achieve great things by unlocking our residue of childish wonder, the way things made our souls sing so much more vibrantly back then: our Christmas or birthday feeling, our manifold excitements in anticipation of what appear (to adult eyes) fairly mundane outings and ventures. And scale is one way of doing this. When we are little, the world around is big. When we grow up it appears to shrink proportionately. Accordingly, when we write fantasy in which items in our world are scaled up again such that our characters assume, in comparison, childish dimensions, one of the things we are doing is reawakening that childish part of ourselves. When done well it can be an immensely effective technique. But to do it well we have to recall that being a tiny child surrounded by gigantic structures and giant-sized lumbering adults was as often alarming and unsettling as it was exciting and adventurous.

SCARINESS

Many writers of fantasy big beasts pay lip service to 'scariness'; but the plain fact is that lip service is not enough. In the *Narnia* books Aslan is as cuddly an oversized house cat as any timid reader could wish for – your secret best friend, only with proper magical powers and a desire to look out for you. From time to time, characters will make reference to Aslan's notionally terrifying sublimity: 'He's not a tame lion, you know,' as Mr Tumnus deflatingly puts it. Except that, in terms of the storytelling, he is. We like our pet house cats to be cheeky and a bit naughty, to have individuality and spirit; but we don't want them actually to scare us. We'd hardly keep them in the house if we did.

What goes for Aslan goes ten times for dragons – at least as dragons are now written. Back in the day (the day in this case being before the Norman Conquest), dragons were genuinely terrifying. The dragon in *Beowulf* caps a tale of increasing terrifyingness – er, terrifyingosity. An increasingly terrifying tale. First the great troll-like man-eater Grendl. Then, even larger and more alarming, Grendl's mother, out for revenge after the hero Beowulf has slain her monstrous son. And finally, after Beowulf has been acclaimed for his fighting spirit and crowned king – after he has ruled long and well and is an old man, the worst terror of all, the great dragon. Tolkien drew on this Dark Age epic for his wyrm Smaug: but even here (and for all that Smaug *is* alarming and scary), a weird process of civilizing diminishment enters into the picture. For Smaug, though ruthless and catastrophic, speaks like an upper-class English gentleman, a member of that caste of perfectly courteous yet sociopathic English aristocrats who established the British Empire. It works, in the novel (another example of this kind of thing is the portrayal of Shere Khan the tiger in Disney's *The Jungle Book*). But it also opens the logic of draconic representation to the chink of humanizing. And with what imaginative shrinkage has that chink been levered open by subsequent writers!

Look at the dragons in fantasy written over the last three decades and you'll be hard pushed to find a properly shivers-in-the-bones scary dragon. In Christopher Paolini's bafflingly popular *Eragon* (2002) and its many sequels, the dragons are big friendly creatures with whom the hero (that's you, reader) has a special bond – a sort of pet horse of larger dimension that can also fly. Anne McCaffrey and Robin Hobb have written multi-volume series in which the dragons are notionally sublime and magnificent but actually big house cats with (of course) a special bond with the hero/heroine – you, dear reader. From *Dragonlance* to *Avatar*, dragons have become our friends, and as such mere ciphers for wish-fulfilment fantasies of power. People look down on me because I'm a geek and physically unprepossessing and live alone with my cats – but they wouldn't laugh if my cat were a 50-foot-long *dragon*!

It's been one of the themes of this volume, and I worry that it will wear smooth with repetition: but I'm going to risk repeating it here. If you are planning on writing a dragon or many dragons into your novel, try to make it fresh. Ask yourself some hard questions. Is the function of your dragon to act as a kind of attack helicopter, with fire-breath instead of sidewinder missiles? Is the dragon an eldritch but essentially a beautiful, lovely, feline creature with whom your main character (that's *you*) has a special, perhaps telepathic, bond? If either of those things obtains, think again.

Dragons are about grandeur, about scale and the sublime. You cannot properly achieve those qualities if every instinct in your writerly soul is straining to reduce them in metaphorical size (no matter how much you stress their notional dimensions) to make them fit to be your special companion.

If you want to write about a magical creature who is the special companion of your main character – do that. If you want to write about grandeur, scale and the sublime, accept that a necessary component of the imaginative effectiveness of those things is terror.

Summary

This chapter has explored seven of the central tropes of science fiction and fantasy, looking at how they have been handled in the past and how they might be treated in new and interesting ways in the future. The seven are:

- *The alien*
- *The spaceship*
- *Psionics*
- *Time travel*
- *Wizards and she-zards*
- *The quest*
- *The dragon.*

Where to next?

The next chapter looks at an absolutely essential part of the writer's technique – revising. Nothing is perfect as it falls straight from the author's keyboard; everything needs to be reworked and improved. Now we'll look at the best ways of going about this.

9

Revising

Writing, the old adage has it, is rewriting. Your first draft is never your best draft. By the same token, your eightieth draft is never your best draft, either. The point when you find yourself obsessively working and reworking, polishing and refining, ripping out paragraphs or whole chapters and starting over – that's the point when you need to stop. Keep in mind one thing: your job is to make what you have written *good*. Your job is not to make it *perfect*. I'm not going to say that perfection is impossible, even in this our sublunary world. But I am going to say that writing is the art of the possible – and that perfectionism is an affliction, a form of writer's block. There are writers who find it almost impossible to let a piece of work go – as if they are being asked personally to leave their house with their hair unbrushed and without any make-up ('But ... but ... people will read my story and see all the imperfections! They will despise me! I will become a laughing stock!').

No, they won't. You are not being asked to produce absolutely flawless work. You are being asked to write as well as you can, given the constraints under which you are working.

Think of it as a balance. A first draft, especially if written in regular, onward-moving sessions, will tend to have certain virtues – energy, flow, immediacy, rawness. It will also contain clumsinesses, typos, daft moments, things that bounce the reader out of her reading experience. Your job is to try to cleanse your draft of these latter things without sacrificing too many of the former. A first draft is not yet good enough to submit to the world – but an eightieth-draft will almost certainly have smoothed all of these edges away and become something inert, over-milled, dead on the page. There comes a time in the process of every writer when s/he has to be like Elsa from *Frozen* and – let it go – let it go-o-o – don't hold it back any more.

How will you know when that moment is? There's no infallible rule, but the following may help:

Get into the habit of thinking of yourself as a writer in it for the longer haul. If you feel that all you have in you is the one 3,000-word story you happen to be writing now – that your whole reputation as a writer depends upon it – then you may start to obsess over it. If, on the other hand, you project forward and think: this is one story, and I want to get it as good as I can in the time I have; but I'm going to go on to write many stories and novels, and at no point will everything depend on any one of them – then you are thinking like a career author..

Get *out* of the habit of thinking that people reading your story will be judging your worth as a human being. They won't. They will be judging the merits of the story itself. One of the advantages of the 'Death of the Author' preached by post-structuralist critics of a Barthean persuasion is that it frees you as a writer from the blocking fear that your ego is on the line with everything you write. It's not. Readers read what you write, not who you are. The good side of this is that you can set aside your ego, and its needy whining, when you're writing and concentrate on the words on the page. The downside is that no reader is going to give bad writing a free pass just because the author is a really nice person. Why should they? But this isn't actually a downside; it's another upside. It is a way of reminding yourself of the difference between being an amateur and a professional.

The real trick to revising well is reading as a reader. That, perhaps, looks tautological, but in fact it is not. It means reading your own writing as if you hadn't written it – reading it over as if it had been written by somebody else, somebody you neither love nor hate. It means taking yourself out of the process, and judging the effectiveness or otherwise of the words on the page.

The surest way of reading like a reader is to leave a long time between finishing your draft and starting your revision. If you finish a story in the morning and immediately start revising, your memory of what you were thinking when you wrote it will still be strong and pungent in your head. 'This is what I meant to do ...' is not a good thought to have when you revise, because that's not how readers encounter what you write.

But it may not be practicable to leave months between writing and revising. You may be working to a deadline; you may not want to lose the momentum you feel in moving the project on.

Raymond Chandler

'Throw up into your typewriter every morning. Clean up every noon.'

Some examples from the world of writing

Not all writers revise this way. Robert Heinlein would check his first draft only very lightly, looking for typos and glaring infelicities of expression; then he would submit the story or novel to an editor and make only such revisions as he or she required. I would not advise this, personally. Editors nowadays, to a much greater degree than used to be the case, are swamped with submissions. A piece that is obviously unfinished is going to deselect itself from their attention almost regardless of its other merits. Besides, Heinlein could really only get away with this because he was Heinlein – one of the most famous names in science fiction. When you get to that stage you can, perhaps, try to do the same. While you're still on the way up, you owe it to yourself, and to maximizing your chances of success, to make your draft as good as possible.

Anthony Burgess worked as follows: he would type a page of his novel, then shove the typewriter to one side and read through what he had written. Only when he was happy with the page in front of him would he go on – if it required many changes he would retype it then and there and add it to his pile of accumulating pages; if it didn't he would simply add it to the pile and move on to the next page. I would not recommend this approach either. Burgess got away with it because he wrote all the time and had reached a level of technical facility with his craft not granted to many mortals. In most writers this strategy would result in a writer's-block-like series of anxious stoppages, and the draft would never acquire any larger fluency. It is also hard to get a sense of the larger structural and architectonic successes of your story if you are only ever revising in discrete, page-long chunks.

At the other end of the scale are those writers who revised and revised. Marcel Proust worked over and over his manuscripts. After the printers had somehow decoded his palimpsest of tangled handwriting and set the novel up in print, they would send the proofs back to him and he would radically revise and change whole passages. Don't do this. Few things annoy publishers as much as having to go to the expense of setting a book up in proof, only to have to set the whole thing up in proof again because the author has changed his/her mind. They will almost certainly bill you for the expense of doing so.

Another example is Tolkien. He did not rewrite his proofs, but he did hang on to his books for a very long time, reworking and revising them. The success of *The Hobbit* in 1937 meant that his publishers encouraged him to write a sequel then and there. That work, *The Lord of the Rings*, wasn't published until 1954–5, in part because Tolkien just took a long time before he thought it was ready. Indeed, in the preface to that great novel he confesses that he was still not happy with it even then: he would have liked to continue revising it, not least to make it longer. Tolkien began writing *The Silmarillion* in the 1920s; he worked and reworked it, and it remained unfinished at his death in 1973 (it eventually appeared posthumously, edited by his son Christopher, in 1977). If you are hoping to write a fantasy, I might diplomatically suggest that you should do so over a timescale rather less dilatory than 57 years.

To come down from the sublime to the ridiculous: what do I do, as a writer?

Well: the part of the process I enjoy most is the writing – the revising is more of a chore. I know writers for whom this is exactly the other way about; they find the initial drafting a burdensome process of pushing their imagination uphill, but enjoy the more defined process of revising that draft.

For me, the process of writing is quite distinct from the process of revising. For the former, the task is to generate a first draft as fluently as possible. I write best in the mornings. I take myself away from distractions (no Internet access; and some coffee shop away from the undone domestic chores of home). I put some music on my headphones, pick up where I left it yesterday and start writing. It may be that I need to work back over the preceding paragraph, or maybe the preceding two, to get my eye in; but I am deliberately not trying to work through previously drafted material – I'm trying to make something new – so I keep this to a minimum. Then I write. Most of all, I consciously ignore the little voice inside my head (we talked about this earlier: that voice that says 'Well, that's not a very good sentence! This story is rubbish! No one's going to want to read this!'). It's not that I don't possess such a voice; it's just that I don't listen to it. I think the music helps in this regard. When I hit my (imperial novelty) groove, the experience is like reading something, but more so – more immersive, more engaging and so on. I'm not worrying at this stage that the draft will be full of errors and horriblenesses, because I know I'm going to go back over it. Some writers I know work to a set word count; others (and this is me) work to a period of time. It's a good idea to pace yourself. Your first two or three hours of writing will tend to produce better material than your seventh and eighth hours.

Revising tends to happen in a different space. I leave as long as possible between drafting and revising: at least a week for a short story, considerably longer for a novel. I tend to revise my stuff in the afternoons and evenings, working through it once or twice to create a smartened text, and then looking quickly over it once again before submitting it to wherever I'm submitting to. I don't listen to music when I revise because I need to concentrate in a different sort of way. The aim in revising is not fluency but accuracy. Revising is less exhilarating than draft-writing, but it is no less necessary.

Two levels of revision

It's good not to overthink the process. Certainly, it's possible to break the process of revision into many layers – to revise each sentence, to consider each paragraph and determine whether it has a pleasing shape, to revise on the level of the scene, of the chapter, of the larger structure. But it's more important to get the revision done than it is to obsess over it, so I'm going to suggest you approach it on two levels.

1 The level of the sentence.

2 The level of the larger structure.

You may find it easier to address '2' first. There's a kind of logic in doing it that way round: after all, revising the larger structure may entail cutting out paragraphs or even whole chapters; and it seems like a waste of time to go through a passage carefully addressing it sentence by sentence, only to chop the whole thing out. That's fine: and (to repeat myself) so long as you actually do the revision and end up with an improved final draft, it doesn't matter what order you do it in.

Nonetheless, I'm going to suggest that you start on the level of the sentence. I suggest this because this is how we encounter stories and novels as readers – we take them one sentence at a time. And the principle of revising is to encounter your own work as a stranger might.

Cutting is hard. Not for nothing do people speak of 'murdering your darlings'. It can feel like homicide to highlight that hard-crafted sentence and press the delete button. But if the surgeon were too squeamish to cut, the patient would die.

I recommend keeping a file open into which you dispose all those sentences and passages that you cut from your draft. That way, you won't feel as if you entirely wasted your time drafting them. Tell yourself whatever you need to tell yourself to enable your inner surgeon. Tell yourself: 'That's a good sentence, a nice simile, a snappy piece of dialogue – I'll keep in it my bits and bobs file and maybe use it for a later story!' It might even be true. Tell yourself: 'OK, so Chapter 13 has to go, it's holding up the whole story. But when my book is published and has sold 15 million copies, I'll issue a sort of "director's cut" version in which fans will gasp with awe over all those sections that hit the cutting-room floor!' This is much less likely to be true, not because you won't go on to sell 15 million copies of your book – after all, who knows? – but because 'director's cut' versions of films are rarely as good as the leaner, more streamlined versions originally released. Our business here is with books, not films, so I'll confine myself to the example of Stephen King. King is a great writer, with a set of extraordinary technical chops. Nonetheless, his original version of his flu apocalypse novel *The Stand* (published in 1978) is considerably better than the bloated, put-back-in-all-the-stuff-my-original-editor-made-me-cut-out re-issue 'author's cut' version of 1990.

Key idea

William Faulkner wrote: 'In writing, you must kill all your darlings.' This may be the most famous piece of writing advice any American author ever uttered. Of course, it needs to be pinched with some salt, and maybe a splash of vinegar too. Many of your darlings will be not only fine but needed for the story. The force of Faulkner's line, though, is that you should not become personally attached to any particular thing you wrote. Such attachment is a kind of vanity, an index to how clever you think yourself, and writers must jettison such pride. Your writing must serve the story, not your ego.

Tell yourself that no writing is ever wasted. Just by writing it, you have practised and therefore improved your craft. You can tell yourself this.

There's another reason why you may feel disinclined to cut stuff out, and that's a suspicion that you can't afford to waste anything. At root, this is the fear that you won't ever again have a good story idea. You will. One purpose of this book is to show how easy it is to generate new ideas and new ways of phrasing and expressing those ideas. You can relax.

Sentences

Take each of your sentences in turn. Read it and check for the sorts of problems we identified in earlier chapters, including the following.

GRAMMATICAL AND SYNTACTICAL ERRORS

Make sure that every sentence has at least a subject and a verb, and (more often) a subject, verb and object. Make sure the sentence agrees internally as to number ('The elf maidens was beautiful' is wrong) and tense ('The wizard was wearing a blue robe, and he walks briskly up the steps' is wrong).

STRUCTURAL UNGAINLINESS

In particular, watch for long, sprawling sentences. You may opt for these, of course, as a deliberate aesthetic strategy; there's precedence for it in works by writers like Thomas Pynchon and David Foster Wallace. But it's very easy to write this sort of sentence badly, and surprisingly hard to write it well. Broadly, you should watch out for what is called 'comma splicing', linking separate clauses with commas. Here's an example of a single sentence from fantasy stylist Robert Jordan: 'The stream of people flowing the other way was mostly Seanchan, soldiers in ordered ranks, with their segmented armour, painted in stripes, and helmets that looked like the heads of huge insects, some marching and some mounted nobles, nobles who were always mounted, wearing ornate cloaks, pleated riding dresses and lace veils, and voluminous trousers and long coats.' This – from 2003's *Crossroads of Twilight* – gives the impression of having been jotted down as it occurred to the author, ticking off the elements as they paraded past his inner eye. That's fine for a rough draft; but it is sprawly and ugly in a finished draft.

PRECISION AND CONCISION

Vagueness is no good ('Elfie looked like a hero. He rode his hero's mount through the nice-looking landscape'). But dwelling on too much inconsequential detail can be boring – if you set out to tell your reader absolutely everything about a given scene, you are not only trespassing on her patience, you are robbing her imagination of its proper partnership in the reading experience. Better to write 'Robert made himself a cup of tea' than to write 'Robert filled the kettle and flicked the switch; while it began heating the water he retrieved a black mug from the cupboard and dropped a teabag inside. He waited. When the kettle began spouting its great gouts of steam, he etc., etc., etc.'

You take my point.

Robert Jordan (him again) once wrote the sentence: 'This fire was not at all small, and the room seemed not far short of hot, a welcome heat that soaked into the flesh and banished shivers' (it's in *Knife of Dreams* from 2005). Look at that sentence. Tell me honestly in what ways it is preferable to the sentence 'A large fire warmed the room.' This is not precision; it is mere finicky fussing. Quite apart from anything else – 'the room seemed not far short of hot, a welcome heat that soaked into the flesh and banished shivers'? I ask you. As opposed to a heat that 'bounces off the flesh and chills the very bones'? Because that's not the sort of heat you want from an open fire. No, indeed.

To shift genres: Robert Ludlum once wrote the sentence, 'His eyes slid down her dress.' If you should ever find that you have written such a sentence – don't panic. It can happen to the best of us. The important thing is not that you wrote it, but that you spotted it during your revision. Change it, rewrite it, alter it, and above all make sure that your reader is not faced with the queasy thought of eyeballs, slimy in their own blood, slipping hideously down a woman's dress while she (presumably) screams in horror. Ludlum means that the male protagonist glances admiringly at the heroine's dress. If that's what you mean – then say that.

CLICHÉ

These inevitably slip through. Be merciless with them: as Martin Amis once said, the prime job of a writer should be to wage war on cliché. Either alter your clichéd phrase for one that is more vivid or evocative (although not for one that is outlandishly trying too hard), or else mark it for later revision.

DIALOGUE

When revising your dialogue, read it aloud. You may feel a little foolish doing this, but it's an invaluable way of testing it for falsity or clumsiness.

Make sure that your characters don't simply decant everything that is in their (or your) mind into speech. People don't simply say what they are thinking.

Make sure your characters aren't 'as-you-know-Bobbing' one another. Character A should not be telling Character B something s/he already knows just to get the reader up to speed.

The structural level

It can be a good idea to make a map of your novel, listing every scene and adding a brief description of what happens in it. You need to pay particular attention to two things: the structural arrangement of events and the logic of POV.

Where the former is concerned, you need to make sure you have a beginning, a middle and an end; that the intensity or drama of scenes works (for instance that quieter or more expository scenes are layered, like parfait, between more action-based or climactic moments, rather than having the first half your novel the former and the second half the latter). In a regular novel of 90,000 words or so, you'll have space for perhaps seven or eight really key scenes: an opening that grabs the reader; an incident that gives momentum to the main plot; an end-of-act-I-type scene; a midpoint highlight; an end-of-act-II-type scene; a major reversal scene; a bounce-back climax; a wrapping up. Sketching your larger structure will give you a sense of whether all these are present and correct.

With POV, you need to ensure that the shifts between different characters' points of view do not confuse or wrong-foot the reader. She needs to be able to move smoothly from Character A's POV to Character B's (or as many different POVs as you have decided upon). To this end, don't chop and change POV too often. It's rarely a good idea to keep swapping POV within one chapter, for example. And be aware that a reader who has been excitedly reading Character M's point-of-view adventures will feel a jolt, perhaps of disappointment, to turn to the next chapter and find that she now has to focus her attention on Character Z's instead. It can be good to structure your book with cliffhanger chapter endings, but you'll also need to be aware that readers may feel grumpy at being denied the satisfactions of closure. Make your new POV instantly intriguing and relevant.

Readers read for characters and the things that happen to them. Writers, often, write to realize their plot, and use characters to make the plot happen. Revision is when you can shift your emphasis from the latter to the former.

One thing to watch for, above all, is characters acting out of character just so that your exciting or ingenious plot can move forwards.

I'll give you an example from the popular HBO TV drama *Game of Thrones*. Now, generally speaking, the screenwriters have done a superb job of adapting George R.R. Martin's marvellous but sprawling novels for the small screen. They have, in point of fact, done precisely what a good reviser should do – they have trimmed and focused, made leaner and more purposeful. No scene in the TV series is superfluous; every one either moves the story on or else adds relevance and depth to our understanding of the characters. But the adaptors have also added scenes, knowing that each episode must include dramatic and arresting moments.

In the novels, the crippled son of Ned Stark, Bran, is carried north of the great wall by his simple-minded servant Hodor, guided by a brother and sister. His father mother and brother have been killed and his family home destroyed; only his two sisters (far to the south) and his half-brother Jon Snow (in the Night's Watch, guarding the great ice wall) remain alive. Bran has magical abilities that will prove vital to the eventual working out of the over-arching plot of the novels; but in the printed form he does little more than trek across the snowy wilderness. In the TV series, in order to inject a little more drama, Bran and his companions are captured north of the wall by some dangerous Black Watch deserters. Jon Snow leads a band of loyal Black Watch guardians to eliminate this little mutinous band, happening upon them while Bran and his friends are tied up.

This whole scene isn't in the original novel, and although including it in the TV serial makes a kind of sense, it also introduces problems. The main one is this: Jon Snow kills the rebel Night's Watchmen; and Bran knows that he has come. Wouldn't Bran be happy to be reunited with his brother?

This can't happen, though, because then Bran would be carried south of the wall again, and Martin's novels require him to go further into the north. So, what happens in the episode (Series 4, Episode 5, 'First of His Name', if you're counting) is that Bran's companion, Jojen, overrules Bran's desire to see his brother again. This doesn't work, because it puts the exigencies of plotting over the plausibility of character. Jojen in effect is saying: 'You mustn't reveal to your brother that you're even here, because he will prevent you from going further north, and we need to go north because of some underpowered notional explanation that has something to do with a three-eyed-raven'; and this is not enough…

Summary

This chapter has been all about the absolute necessity of revising your work. Never just bundle up a first draft, send it off to an editor and hope for the best. We discussed two main authorial models of revision:

1 *Revising as you go along, either page by page, or revising the previous day's output before starting on today's, or else chapter by chapter.*

2 *Revising as a distinct phase, separated from writing by as much time as possible. This is my own preferred mode of working.*

You need to find out for yourself which gets the best effects for you – so long as you do revise.

It's useful to think of revision on two main levels, checking through sentence by sentence, and reading through with an eye on the coherence and effectiveness of the larger structure of the story.

Check your prose sentence by sentence for grammatical and syntactical errors; for too-sprawling and onrolling syntax; for imprecision and prolixity generally; and for cliché – extirpate this latter without remorse. Read your dialogue aloud to yourself to see how it sounds.

While you are doing this, you will start to get a sense of how well the larger elements of your storytelling and structure are working.

Where to next?

We have worked through the elements of originating, developing and writing a science-fiction or fantasy idea. Revision is the final step in that process.

What's next is to get your work published. The next chapter explores the various options before you, from self-publishing to getting a traditional publisher interested, and promoting and selling the work. And, just as important, coping with being published!

10

<_Getting published

You have worked long, and invested your heart's blood, in finishing your novel or story. Naturally, you want to publish it.

I'd like to say that if your writing is good enough it will get published. Once upon a time I think that may even have been true – your job was to write the best book you could and then put it on the market – and if the book was good and you kept it on the market long enough, it would sell. I'm not sure that is the case any longer.

Once upon a time, self-publishing was tantamount to an admission of failure. E-books have changed all that. Now many writers circumvent the process of traditional publishing altogether, established names as well as neophytes. Hugh Howey started out by self-publishing e-versions of his SF novels, and enjoyed such success with them that he was picked up by a traditional publisher and became an international bestseller.

If that's your dream, then: bravo. Be advised, though, that for every such case there are hundreds of earnest, driven writers who enjoy modest success or no success at all.

Traditional publishing

Speaking for myself, though I have dabbled in self-publishing ebooks, I am a veteran of the traditional route. Almost all my books have been published by Victor Gollancz (part of Orion Books, themselves part of the Hachette Publishing multinational). Gollancz is one of the main SF/fantasy imprints in the UK (there are several others, including Orbit and HarperCollins), and for my money they have the most exciting list – of course, you'd expect me to say so! I can report that they have treated me well.

 Key idea

Here's what *not* to do. Do not simply send off your manuscript to a big-name publisher unsolicited. If you do that, they will put it on the slush pile (or park it in a slush-pile folder on the computer if it's an electronic submission). Once every hundred years or so, publishers send in work-experience bods to browse the huge pyramid of slush-pile paperwork for half an hour. It is vanishingly rare that any work so submitted actually gets accepted.

Here's what to do instead: either get an agent (google 'literary agencies' or check out *The Writers' & Artists' Yearbook* – your local public library will have a copy – for the lists of UK and US agents); or do some research to find out who is who in the publisher you're interested in and send them a brief, polite letter explaining what your book is about and why it is distinctive. If – and only if – the editor replies positively, with a request for a complete outline or perhaps even with a request to see the whole thing, should you send stuff on. More about agents and the practical process of working with publishers below.

With a traditional publisher, you get:
- the imprimatur of a proper press
- an editor
- professional production and design
- publicity, marketing and sales
- warehousing and shipping
- royalties, and perhaps an advance.

THE IMPRIMATUR OF A PROPER PRESS

This counts for a great deal. Whatever else they do, traditional publishers are increasingly gatekeepers in the citadel of content (horrid word) – sifting the great press of a million unpublished, self-published or online stories and novels to extract the worthwhile, the readable and the good. If a reader picks up a published book, at least they know it has passed a basic test of worth. One person, and in practice several people, have read it and deemed it worth publishing. If you click to download somebody's self-published story, it could be marvellous but is much more likely to be drek. Publishers filter out the drek.

AN EDITOR

Proper publishing involves having an experienced industry professional going over your work and giving you feedback. My experience is that this part of the process is invaluable: my own writing has benefited immensely and repeatedly from the input of my editor (it helps that he is also now a friend of mine). The editor's job is to make the book as good as it can be.

PROFESSIONAL PRODUCTION AND DESIGN

Publishers employ several layers of staff to turn your word file into an attractive and saleable final product – copy-editors, proofreaders, designers and artists. We all know we should not judge a book by its cover, but we all do that anyway; and a really good cover makes a calculable difference in terms of sales. Indeed, one of the things that separates out professional publishing from self-publishing is that the latter too often have laughably amateur, incompetent cover art!

PUBLICITY, MARKETING AND SALES

Most publishers, and all the larger ones, employ publicity personnel whose job is to raise the profile of your book – to get it reviewed and noticed, to arrange for you to be interviewed, to do readings and appear at conventions. They will also try to build you as a brand, to talk to bookshops, supermarkets and online retailers about getting your book on the shelves.

WAREHOUSING AND SHIPPING

If we are talking about physical copies of books, then they take up space (which isn't free) and must be moved about (which also isn't free). A publisher looks after all this side of things for you.

MONEY

Last but certainly not least: professional publishers will pay you a royalty on each copy of your book that is sold. They may also pay you an advance against royalties (see below). They will also take a cut themselves, of course – but publishers are a business, not a charity, and need to make money in order to remain viable.

 Key idea: day jobbing

The Society of Authors is the UK organization for professional writers – the stress, there, being on the 'professional': you have to earn money by your writing to be eligible. They recently surveyed their members and discovered that the average annual earnings of a writer were a touch over £4,000. That's the average: some authors earn a lot more than that; many earn less. If you're there or thereabouts, earnings-wise, and you fancy doing more than living in your parents' spare room and eating cat food out of a tin, you'll need to give serious thought to acquiring a day job. I have a day job myself, to help cover the mortgage and put shoes on my kids' ever-growing feet – I teach creative writing and literature at the University of London. The main consideration with such employment must, of course, be: will it leave me time and energy to write?

Royalties

A typical royalty deal will be between 7 and 12 per cent – if you're offered much less than this, you might want to think about approaching someone else. An exception is the big supermarkets, who typically agree to take large numbers of books but only at a larger than usual discount: in these circumstances it's usually worth your while to accept a lower royalty and for the publisher to take a smaller overhead, since the numbers of books sold can be very large. You're unlikely to be able to negotiate a larger royalty unless you're already a super-seller. Royalties are calculated not against the retail price printed on the book, but against the net receipt – the amount left after the bookseller has taken their cut. This can be anything up to 50 per cent and sometimes more. For example, a paperback retailing in the shop at £8.99 might return a net receipt to the publisher of 45 per cent – £4.05. If your royalty deal is 10 per cent, this means that for every copy the bookshop sells you get 40 pennies and one ha'penny. That doesn't sound much, but it scales up. If you sell a modest but respectable 1,000 copies, you'd earn £405. If you sell the harder-to-reach but achievable 10,000 copies you'd earn £4,050. And so on. Royalty rates on ebooks are generally higher, but the retail price of e-ooks is generally lower, so it balances out.

Other income

Royalties from sales of individual copies of your book aren't the only way you can earn money through your writing; and a professional publisher can help you realize some of the alternatives. For example, you can sell overseas and translation rights. In the case of the latter, overseas publishers are buying the right to publish your books in their territories: in addition to all the regular costs of publishing they may also have to pay a translator (translators are the great unsung heroes of the publishing world and they are ludicrously underpaid – but any money they do receive is in the end going to come out of your rights deal).

For another example, you can sell film rights. A lot of writers dream of a fat film deal and some few have been made rich by them, but for most the reality is rather more mundane. In the first instance, a production company may pay for an 'option' – the exclusive right to develop your book into a film project over a set period (12 months, say). They may then hire a scriptwriter and talk to producers about raising the money actually to make the film. Most books that are 'optioned' proceed no further than this, and the sums paid for an option are generally pretty modest. If you get to the next stage you may sign an actual film deal, and perhaps get a little more money, but generally speaking you won't get any serious money until the first day of actual filming. Perhaps one in a hundred books optioned eventually ends up getting made into a motion picture, so don't set your hopes too high. Other sources of income for the published writer include the ALCS, the organization that gathers fees for copyright usage, and PLR, which pays you a small sum every time a copy of your book is taken out of the library.

 ## Key idea: is an agent a shield?

Should you get an agent? If you're starting out it's certainly worth thinking about. The downside is that agents cost – they'll take between 10 and 15 per cent of the money you earn as their cut and, as with anyone you pay to work for you, it's worth making sure that you're getting value for money. The upside is that publishers are more likely to pay attention to an agent than to a previously unpublished author on their own – if a book is good enough to interest an agent, the publisher knows that it won't be drek. And a good agent is more than just a foot in the publisher's door: s/he will give you feedback on your writing and help you improve it, and s/he can offer professional advice on contracts. S/he can also be a professional friend, listening to your complaints, offering advice and generally being supportive. Mind you, it can be as hard getting a good agent as getting a publisher. Google for agents in your territory; get the most recent *Writers' & Artists' Yearbook* (you can buy it or refer to it in your local public library) and scan the list of agents it contains – these will specify whether they're interested in genre or not, and whether they have any spaces. Be polite; contact and follow up.

Short fiction

The Internet has changed the market for short stories perhaps more than any other aspect of the writer's life. It used to be possible for a suitably prolific genre author to draw down a reasonable living just from writing shorts – back in the 1930s, or even in the 1960s, there were dozens of pro-rate-paying magazines like *Amazing Stories* and *Astounding/Analog* eager for good new content. Philip Dick lived for most of the 1960s, for example, more or less off his short-story income. That's no longer the case. Most of the old magazines have gone bust; those few that still exist (*Amazing* and *Analog* still publish; there's also *Interzone* in the UK; and some online journals – *Clarkesworld* and *Strange Horizons* for instance – pay for content) are all oversupplied with submissions. It is possible to sell stories to them, but not for very much money, and it's not easy.

What's different is the competition. Millions of free words are published every single day online; articles, reviews, stories, poems – a Niagara of content pouring into every smartphone and iPad on the planet. Most of it is rubbish, of course; but a lot isn't – and it's all competing for the same eyeballs that could be reading your fiction. Why should a reader pay to buy the magazine with your story in it, when she can pick up stories just as good for free?

I don't mean to be too negative. And since we're talking, in this chapter, about the practicalities of publishing it's worth noting that short stories are an excellent discipline for a writer. You have to establish your premise, set your characters in motion, run through the action and resolve everything in short order: writing shorts helps tone your writerly muscles. And it can make good sense, in terms of building your reputation as a writer, to publish a string of good short stories before you essay your first novel-length piece. Alastair Reynolds and Greg Egan, to name two contemporary giants of the scene, built their careers that way. I myself write a great many short stories. I don't tend to do this for magazine markets (I have, for instance, never been able to sell a story to either *Analog* or *Interzone*). What I mostly do is publish in anthologies and collections of original short fiction, a variety of which are still being published each year. These may be themed anthologies, in which case I and other authors are commissioned to write to a particular brief; or they may be general collections. Most are published by small presses, and one of the glories of the SF and fantasy publishing scene is how many small presses it contains. The downside is that the fees for contributing are not, generally, high: £50 per story is common. You have to decide whether the time you invest in writing a story is being properly remunerated at that rate.

Self-publishing

The bottom line is that the publishers are a business, not a charity. They need to make money or they will go under; and they make their money by piggy-backing on the financial success of their authors. It's not wholly mercenary – most publishers are happy to publish writers who make only modest returns in order to diversify their lists, and most editors are more interested in good writing than in the commercial bottom line. But that bottom line never goes away, and no commercial press can afford to keep publishing a writer who consistently loses money. The deal they offer is: we take our cut, and in return you get all the benefits listed above.

Of course, if you self-publish, then the only person who takes a cut from your sales is you. *If* (it's a big if) you sell a lot, this can mean a healthy chunk of money. The downside is that by self-publishing you are agreeing to work both as author and publisher, and if this only doubles your workload then you're lucky.

That said, many writers are happy to do it this way. This is what it means in practical terms (to revisit the list from above):

IMPRIMATUR

A fancy name ('Prestige Science Fiction Publishing') and even an elaborate logo are no substitute for an established reputation publishing excellent science fiction and fantasy, and the readers know it. Your best bet as a self-publisher by way of signalling to the market that your writing is not drek is probably endorsements – and to get these you need a degree of cheek that some folk are less comfortable with. What it means is getting established names in the genre to blurb your book, and what *that* means is asking them to read it and say nice, quotable things. There are several ways of going about this, of which 'emailing the most famous writer you can think of out of the blue via their author website and begging them to read your 800-page unpublished space opera' is probably the least advisable. I don't want to sound too negative here: all established writers remember how hard it was starting out, and many are keen to pay back and help up-and-coming talent. But established writers are also time poor, overworked and deadline-harassed individuals, often juggling writing and day jobs (see above), who receive many more requests to blurb and review than there are hours in the day. I'm not all that famous, even within science fiction, and I get requests like this all the time, many from established publishers trying to give their first-time authors an extra boost. I do what I can, but the moral of the story is: be reasonable. If 'famous author' politely declines your request, or even (though this is ruder) simply doesn't answer your email, it may not be because they are the worst human being in the world. It will help if you build some kind of relationships first: follow your favourite writers on Twitter, go to SF conventions and buy them a beer. They'll be more likely to look favourably on your requests then – though they still may be too hard pressed to help.

AN EDITOR

This is the real crunch: self-publishing means being your own editor. This is harder than it looks, not only because actual editors are skilled and experienced professionals who know what they are doing, but because one key advantage an editor brings is a fresh pair of eyes. Even if you have some of the skills of the former, you cannot by definition have the latter. It may be that you can persuade boyfriend, girlfriend, husband or wife to act as unofficial editor by reading and critiquing your manuscript, though such people will almost certainly soft-peddle their criticisms because, you know, they have to live with you afterwards. Or you could get outsiders to read your work. But there's an ethical as well as a practical concern here. For myself I believe workers should be paid for their work; and just as I wouldn't expect my plumber friend or my carpenter friend to fix my central heating or build me a wardrobe for free just because they are my friend, I wouldn't expect somebody to provide a professional edit on my book for nothing. Luckily there are people who work as freelance editors, many of them with experience in professional publishing. The downside is that they cost but, as with many things, in life you get what you pay for.

PROFESSIONAL PRODUCTION AND DESIGN

Design is another area where, in my experience, it is worth paying for the input of professionals. Your pencil and watercolour sketch of a spaceship achieving orbit may look OK; your photograph of a misty forest at dawn may look Celtic and magical on your iPhone; but with a Comic Sans title and author name layered over the top and printed on to the cover of the finished product, it *will* look lame. Photoshop is harder to use than you think. I published a novella as an ebook via Amazon; and while I edited and proofread the text myself, I bit the bullet and paid a professional artist £100 to design the cover. Of course, this meant that when I finally totted up the amount selling the book online brought in, subtracted this cost and divided the remainder by the hours I had spent on the project, the resulting sum was a tiny fraction of the UK national minimum wage. But that's the way it goes.

PUBLICITY, MARKETING AND SALES

Letting the world know about your book is not an easy business. You can set up websites, blogs and Twitter accounts and send out blanket emails urging people to buy a copy, but this practice has a name, and the name is spam. People don't like getting spammed – you don't like it yourself. So what to do? Here I'd suggest *not* paying for adverts: I'm not convinced anybody sees a poster for a book and thinks to themselves, 'Yes, I will buy this book'. In point of fact, there are three things that sell books: (a) word of mouth (because if somebody I know says to me, 'Hey, this book is really great, you should read it!' I'm likely to seriously consider it: after all, they know me); (b) celebrity – people will buy books by famous people, from memoirs to novels, regardless of quality (though 'becoming a soap-opera actor, rock star or international film icon' is probably too roundabout a way of getting a publishing contract for most people); and (c) nobody knows! There are books that become bestsellers, often from a standing start, while myriad other, better books completely fail to dent the market, and nobody knows why. Professional publishers don't know why – if they did, then they would publish only those books. Now, 'word of mouth' cannot be faked; and celebrity is beyond our reach; but the third thing may still work in your favour!

WAREHOUSING AND SHIPPING

If your self-publishing involves generating actual physical books, then you will have to deal with the practical difficulties entailed. Short of buying, housing and running an actual printing press and binding machine, this means in the first instance paying a printer to manufacture the actual books. It also means storing them – either paying for a lock-up or space in a storage warehouse, or else stacking boxes in your spare room (assuming you have one). It means putting multiple copies of your book into padded envelopes, writing multiple addresses, paying for postage and carrying them down to the post office, to meet the sales you generate via your online presence. It means renting table space at an SF convention and porting many copies of your book to the venue (books are heavy!), hoping that the drifting through-passage of SF fans provides enough actual customers to make it financially worth your while. It means, for some intrepid souls, going into local bookshops and persuading them to give your self-published book shelf space for a set time and an agreed cut of any money made from sales (as above, this cut could easily be more than 50 per cent: high-street bookshops have many expensive overheads to cover, from commercial rents and rates to staff salaries). On the upside, you will have an actual copy of your book, something you can hold in your hand. And some people fall in love with the process of becoming a small press – some even expand and start publishing other people's work.

E-publishing, of course, obviates the need for all this physical storage – although not the need to produce a professional, clean, copy-edited and proofread finished product.

Self-publishing an ebook: an imaginary case study

In this section I'm going to walk through an imaginary case study – that is, a book I've just this minute made up. It's called 'The Stratosphere My Prison'. It's an 80,000-word, future-set prison drama, with a twist in the nature of the prison. In my future society, criminals are fitted with anti-gravity packs, fixed physically to their spines. These are preset such that the wearer can fly no lower than 1,000 metres – additional restraints programmed into the backpack prevent prisoners approaching mountainous areas or bothering planes. The inmate is then provided with a corded harpoon (to catch birds); a sponge belt to soak up water from rain or clouds, and set on their way. They can go anywhere they like, but never again approach human habitation on the ground or come lower than their minimum; the idea being not only to punish them but to serve as a deterrent and continual reminder to ground-dwellers (many of whom follow the inmates with telescopes). The prisoners are often cold, drenched and wretched; and they are forced to eat pigeons and seagulls. The story concerns a new prisoner, sent into the sky protesting his innocence, who quickly learns that some of the other inmates are ready to supplement their meagre diet with something more human. Humanitarian organizations and family members send up treats via hydrogen balloons – an illegal but widespread practice, which results in fierce fighting between prisoners over the spoils. Other less humane individuals like to take pot-shots at low-flying prisoners ...

So: perhaps I have tried to interest an agent or publisher in my book and have been unsuccessful; or perhaps I have decided to self-publish straight away. Either way, I need to produce a clean word file. This means doing the following:

1 **Finalizing the draft,** so that the book reads smoothly, hits the right story beats, develops its characters and generally does all the things the earlier chapters of this 'Get Started in ...' book have discussed.

2 **Proofreading the finished product.** Typos in any book, hard-copy or e-, are an insult to the reader. Why should she pay good money for a text full of errors? That said, proofreading is a laborious and tricky process. The eye glides over errors, especially if that eye is already over-familiar with the text through multiple rewritings and drafts. There's nothing to be said here but work slowly, carefully, sentence by sentence. I have a friend who claims to proofread their work by reading it backwards (because then they are not distracted by the sense of the writing, and can focus just on the individual words). I've not tried this myself; and though it sounds immensely taxing, it should at least result in a clean text. (Word to the wise: do not rely on your computer spellchecker to proof your document, or you could find that you are talking about asses when you meant assess and cocks when you mean clocks.)

3 **Finalizing the legal necessities:** your copyright notice, asserting your moral right as author, clearing any copyright requirements you may have incurred (see below) and ensuring that what you have written does not infract any laws that obtain in your territory, including libel laws, obscenity laws and laws against incitement to racial or religious hatred.

4 **Sourcing good cover art.**

ROUTES TO PUBLISHING

When this is done, there are three avenues by which I can actually publish my book:

1 **Set up a website.** I could simply set up a website and offer the book for sale as a download file. I'd suggest offering a variety of formats (pdf, mobi and so on) and choosing a realistic price. The advantage here is that you clear all the money you take in from sales, minus only production costs. Let's say I offer 'The Stratosphere My Prison' for sale at £2.99. I contacted a freelance designer online, and she charged me £80 for a nice cover (sunset skyscape with a lone figure silhouetted against the clouds; the title and my name in smartly understated font). I have set up my website so that people can pay either via a credit card or through Paypal, which both add a small marginal cost at the point of transaction; and the site itself is a commercial template bought online. Total costs: £105 (plus a small fraction of each for each transaction processing the money), not counting my time. This means that I need sell only 37 copies of my book to break even; every sale beyond that is pure profit. The downside is: why should anybody buy my book? How do they even know my website is there? How do I drive traffic to my site, and will doing this cost me more money?

2 **Sell through Amazon.** Now there are many people who have problems with Amazon, from their monocrop scorched-earth sales strategies on down. But they do make the business of self-publishing easy. Go to the Amazon 'Kindle direct publishing' site https://kdp.amazon.com/ and register. Downsides include that you must pay the company a cut and that you are locked in to Amazon's pricing policy. Provided you're happy to price your book at the level Amazon thinks right, that means you could take away a 70-per-cent royalty, which is another way of saying that Amazon will take a 30-per-cent cut. These terms, though, are less generous if you don't want to charge what Amazon thinks you should be charging. On the upside, Amazon is the globe's single biggest bookshop, and you are putting your book on the shelf in a place where the whole world shops. On the downside, you are putting your book on a shelf alongside literally millions of other books; so you still need to find a way of drawing the attention of interested parties to what you are doing.

3 **Sell through a specialist.** There are many non-Amazon ebook retailers out there, and several of these specialize in SF and fantasy titles. Their reach is smaller than Amazon's, but they generally have loyal followings of readers who check their new titles and buy regularly from them. I can personally recommend Wizard's Tower Press http://wizardstowerpress.com/; but there are plenty of other SF- and fantasy-oriented ebook publishers and online stores out there worth checking out, including Scorpius Digital Publishing http://www.scorpiusdigital.com/; and Double Dragon E-books Inc http://www.double-dragon-ebooks.com/.

PUBLICITY

So, 'The Stratosphere My Prison' is out there. Now I have to publicize it.

- I email everybody in my address book telling them the book has been published. This is, technically, spam; and nobody likes getting spammed – but at least it is not an offer of Nigerian Viagra. Still, I'll probably only get away with this because the people in my address book are my friends. (On the downside: friends and family might expect a free copy of your book – they're you're friends and family, after all.) I probably wouldn't get away with spamming strangers.

- I set up a Twitter account @STRATOSPHEREMYPRISON and tweet about the book. Once again, you already know what it's like to be on the receiving end of commercial tweet-spam, and it's annoying. At the very least, do more with your Twitter feed than just plug your book. Tweet witty and perceptive things, link to other people's writing as well as your own, and acquire a following by not seeking merely to exploit people.

- I approach a few friends and, swallowing my pride and overcoming my natural diffidence, ask them to blurb the book. Most are too busy, but a couple agree. I decided ahead of time not to use Mum or my spouse for this job (no reader is going to be persuaded to buy a book because it has 'A five-star masterpiece!' The Author's Mother on the front cover). But if I write to J.K. Rowling ('Hi, you don't know me, but I've written and am now self-publishing a novel. Please read it and provide me with a positive blurb by next Thursday. Thank you!) I'm willing to bet that, politely or otherwise, she would decline.

- I send a few polite emails to genre sites that review new fiction, and perhaps to a few print publications as well, offering review copies. The protocol here is: they are under no obligation to accept; and even if they do accept they are under no obligation to write a positive review. You might have the cojones to splash 'Improbable conceit, stiffly written, 1.5 stars out of 5' SF MASTHEAD REVIEWS on the front of your book; but I wouldn't.

But let's say I get some good reviews. Let's say I get shortlisted for a genre prize, or pick up some other signs of esteem. Let's say Amazon reader reviews average on the positive side. Maybe sales start to accumulate. What next?

Coping with being published

How-to guides sometimes, and for obvious reasons, treat 'getting published' as the finish line. Some few will include advice on what to do afterwards that is, broadly, practical. And practical advice is not a bad idea. If you start earning money from your writing, you will have to do things like pay tax and National Insurance or your country's equivalent on it; you will have to think about writing the follow-up (a sequel? a new stand-alone?) and building your author brand.

But there's another side to the post-publication life, and it's the emotional one.

I have published 15 novels, two collections of short fiction, various novellas and novelettes and many critical studies and academic works. I am, by any metric, an old hand at this. Nevertheless, I am still a gibbering wreck in the immediate aftermath of publication. I dread reviews: the good ones seem to me pasty and point-missing; the bad ones sear their every word into the tender skin of my brain like a particularly elaborate red-hot cattle brand. I long ago gave up checking my Amazon sales rankings (when I realized that the options were never to check them, or else to reload the page every ten minutes all through every single day); and it's rarely a good idea to see what Amazon reviewers or the Goodreads cognoscenti make of my efforts.

Science fiction is probably a more forgiving environment for the author than other genres. It is, after all, an actual community: a group of people who genuinely care about their beloved genre, and who make the effort to check out what new stuff is emerging. The problem 'literary fiction' authors have (and I'm friends with several) is getting noticed at all: many such books are simply never reviewed and sales in the low hundreds are not uncommon. Science fiction and fantasy is better than this; many online and print venues exist for reviews, we are well supplied with prizes and year's-bests lists, and all of this helps. There may be a downside, though: fans can be surprisingly brutal. Not all SF fans are Sheldon Cooper types, and not all are Comic Book Guy from *The Simpsons* either ('The Stratosphere My Prison? Worst. Sky-prison. Novel. *Ever*!'). But there may be, shall we say, a bias that way. After my first novel was published, I went to a SF convention and found myself at the launch party of someone else's book. I was chatting with a pleasant guy for a while and we swapped names. 'You're Adam Roberts?' he said. 'Didn't you just have a novel published?' I modestly conceded that it was true. 'Wait, it was called *Salt*, wasn't it? I read that! I read that book.' Smiling faintly, I expressed the timid hope that he had enjoyed it. 'Not at all,' he said, benignly. 'No, I hated it. I really hated it. I'll *tell* you a book I read recently that I *really* liked – China Miéville's book. Have you read that? *That's* a really good novel!' As my soul withered inside me like the Wicked Witch of the West at the end of *The Wizard of Oz*, I agreed that Mr Miéville's novel was indeed a contemporary masterpiece. My interlocutor had no sense that he had said anything untoward.

And perhaps he hadn't. Once a book has been published it becomes the property of the world. It's a tricky metamorphosis for the author to manage, but a necessary one. The mistake too many writers make is confusing criticism of their writing with criticism of their worth as human beings. My new friend was clear that he disliked my book, not that I was a piece of scum who had no right to breathe on God's clean earth. The confusion between these two categories was mine, not his.

So that's the first and perhaps most important lesson to learn, post-publication: don't take it personally. It's hard, much harder than you might think – because your book is the child of your mind and imagination, it carried your blood in its metaphorical veins. Still: you are not the same thing as your book. Even very good writers can write rubbish books – Martin Amis wrote *Yellow Dog*; Gene Wolfe wrote *An Evil Guest*.

BAD REVIEWS

Here's what to do with a bad review. (You'll often know you have gotten a bad review ahead of time, because kind friends will be eager to let you know. But even if you stumble across one by chance, this rule obtains.) *Read the review once, right through. Then put it aside and never read it again.* If you never read the review, your own imagination will construct a shadowy monster version of what the review might have said that will be far more destructive and self-esteem-shattering than the actual review. By the same token, if you read bad reviews over and over, obsessively dwelling on every criticism, you'll drive yourself mad. Read it once, and put it aside. Remember that the reviewer is not God, not infallible; but also remember that she is almost certainly not motivated by personal animus and that you can learn, grow and improve from considering their critique. Keep in mind the words of the old song: if you get it wrong, you get it right next time.

Under no circumstances – never, ever, no, nuh-huh, don't even think about it – *reply* to a bad review. Don't vent. Never strike back. Don't email the reviewer in fury; don't post your own take-down of the wickedness and maliciousness of the reviewer. Doing this will bring misery and dishonour down upon your own head, and achieve nothing whatsoever. If the desire to retort burns within you such that you can't get past it, then write it out and stow it away somewhere safe (it's worth doing this, actually, just to give yourself the experience of pulling your bitter retort twelve months later and getting a proper sense of perspective on how transitory such hurt is). But better yet: ignore the desire altogether.

MAINTAINING YOUR WRITING CAREER

Maintaining a career in writing, in a nutshell, boils down to doing four things:

1 **You must stay productive – but not too productive.**
   You want to aim for the middle ground here, neither over-saturating the market with dozens of novels every year until readers grow sick of the very sight of your name; nor leaving decade-long gaps between your writing so that readers forget that you even exist. Write every day, so that writing becomes a habit.

2 **Cultivate good working relationships.**
   This means industry professionals who might commission
   work from you: editors and publishers. Treat them always with
   courtesy; always meet your deadlines; always write to the spec
   you have been given.

3 **Cultivate your fan base.**
   Run a blog and set up a Facebook page and Twitter account,
   aiming to do more with all three than just plugging your work.
   Be charming online: intelligent, witty, perceptive, informative.
   Set aside time to respond to fan emails and messages. Engage in
   the community, go to conventions and literary festivals, stay up
   to speed. Fans are the ones who buy your writing, and there's no
   reason they should do that if you treat them with contempt.

4 **Most of all – you must stay psychologically healthy.**
   Writing is an unusual career in that it is so egregiously inward.
   A writer spends most of her working life tapping at a computer,
   living in her own head. No matter how shy and retiring you are,
   it is not good for you to spend too long like this. The Internet
   is as much a danger as a release where this is concerned: online
   contact with other people is contact, but it is not psychologically
   reliable contact. The web is really a hall of distorting mirrors, in
   which every snarky comment and bad review casts monstrous
   spectres over us. If you are determined to make writing your life,
   then you need to make a deal with yourself, to get out of your
   own head for a certain portion of the day. Hang out with friends;
   interact fully and properly with your partner; play with your
   kids; go for a walk in the sunshine. It's all right. The writing will
   still be there when you get back.

Summary

This chapter has aimed to set out some of the practicalities of publishing. We started with some of the advantages of the traditional route – putting your book in the hands of an established publisher, and thereby gaining:

- *the imprimatur of a proper press*
- *an editor*
- *professional production and design*
- *publicity, marketing and sales*
- *warehousing and shipping*
- *royalties, and perhaps an advance.*

The cost of this is that the publishers will take a share of the money your book earns; and the problem with it (surrendering a cut of your money aside) is that reputable publishers are, without exception, swamped with many more submissions than they could possible print. You may want to consider getting an agent to increase the likelihood of a publisher taking you seriously.

We also considered the situation with self-publishing, either organizing the printing of physical copies of your book, or else publishing ebook-only titles. The advantage here is that you retain complete control, and keep almost all the money you make.

But the disadvantages are that you have to take it upon yourself (or else pay individuals out of your own pocket) to do all the things a professional press would do for you:

- *editing*
- *copy-editing*
- *design and layout*
- *cover art*
- *proofreading*
- *publication*
- *warehousing and shipping*
- *promotion*
- *accounts.*

You may relish these as challenges, or dread them as chores, but they are unavoidable parts of making a book.

Finally, we looked at some of the consequences, both practical and in terms of emotional well-being, of actually getting published. It may be that you earnestly desire to reach that place where such 'problems' become your reality, and will take them as a small price to pay for becoming a professional, published author. And if so, I can only hope: may your wish come true!

What's next?

What's next? Why, what's next is for you to go write your masterpiece. Away with you!

Appendix: SF Plotto

The Plotto is divided into five sections:

1. Characters/actors/agents (pick as many as you like)
2. Premises (pick any ONE)
3. Development directions (pick any ONE)
4. Strophe (the 'turning point' in the three-act structure: pick as many of these as you like, bearing in mind that you will need to string the turns together in a meaningful way, and that while readers love twists, too many will tend to alienate them)
5. Denouement (pick ONE).

The longest section, obviously, is 2; and it can be extended indefinitely with any ideas that occur to you, and which you are encouraged to jot down on the endpapers or inside back cover. This will not only act as a useful aide memoire for you, but it will also (when you become a famous writer, and provided you hang on to your copy of the book) result in a very collectable and therefore valuable artefact. The ideas in 2 are all indicative, and may be used freely, remixed or otherwise adapted in any way, or (of course) disregarded, mocked and reviled.

1 CHARACTERS/ACTORS/AGENTS

1. Protagonist. (Traditional structuralism account of storytelling units tend to talk in terms of 'hero'; a less gender-hidebound twenty-first-century society might add 'or heroine'. But this is science fiction/fantasy! We don't need to be bound by these narrow constraints. Consider making your protagonist female, male, trans-gendered, a telepathically linked set of twins; a hive-mind; a superintelligent eel, or anything else that occurs to you.)
2. Sidekick, comic or otherwise
3. Antagonist
4. Helper
5. Distant object of passion
6. Distant object of passion's forbidding parent/guardian
7. A number (from 2 to 12) of more distantly positioned followers or disciples of the hero

8   Dispatcher (the character who makes the lack known and sends the hero off)

9   The donor, who gives the hero some helpful, usually magical object

10 The false hero – takes credit for the hero's actions or tries to marry the love-object

11 The 'Kevin Bacon' character

12 You, yourself, suitably fictionalized.

2 PREMISES

1   Your own, best idea!

2   In the future, criminals convicted of a crime have their brain chemistry altered so that they must serve their sentence with the time-perception of a six-year-old child – such that days seem to last weeks and years are an impossible-to-conceive length of time. An ex-con, driven half mad by his five-year term inside, develops a revenge virus that will have the reverse effect on the general population – days will appear to go past like minutes, and whole years will zip by.

3   A new quantum telescope produces the most accurate resolution of the famous COBE map of cosmic background radiation yet. What in the earlier image appeared to be random splotches of more or less density are now revealed to be the map of the landmasses on the Earth!

4   In a future war, a new weapon is developed that interacts with the moisture in the air to produce a rapidly expanding toxic foam. Overuse produces a chain reaction in which whole regions of the Earth are covered with choking froth to a height of kilometres – it can only be prevented by heating the air to drive all moisture from it. Driven back to the Sahara Desert, a team attempts a last-ditch battle to save the Earth …

5   Time travel is discovered, but going back in time has the unavoidable side effect of scrambling human consciousness and reducing the mind to the level of a baby. In an attempt to circumvent this, a Neo-Nazi Time Institute plans on sending a baby back in time to 1900, implanted with a microchip to guide its growth to adulthood – their plan is that this individual would then find and guide Adolf Hitler, so as to enable him to avoid his historic mistakes and so win World War II. The plan misfires,

and the child arrives in ancient Egypt, where he is discovered by the Pharaoh's daughter floating down the Nile in a basket ...

6 Aliens invade the Earth, but not on the physical plane. These are aliens who exist as engrams of radio-electricity, and they occupy the sphere of radio transmissions, driving out all human communication and computation. Dropped abruptly back to the Stone Age, humanity must unite to find a way to reclaim their radiosphere ...

7 Deep-sea exploration has been aided for decades now by genetically modified seals, capable of withstanding the immense pressures of the ocean trenches, swimming down with lights, cameras and air tanks to feed data back – cheaper and more flexible than manned deep-water submersibles. But something goes wrong: in the Marianas Trench a group of seven deep-seals encounter something (an alien entity? an ancient Earth intelligence previously quarantined from land-life by its environment? the devil himself?) that uplifts their intellect, rendering them canny and malicious. They begin sabotaging deep sea cables, attacking submarines and ships. And now the intellect-uplift is spreading to other marine life ...

8 Following a series of high-profile corruption scandals, a new law makes it compulsory for all holders of high elected public office (Prime Minister, Chancellor of the Exchequer, Foreign Secretary – or, if you prefer, their US or European equivalents) to be surveilled online at all times, without exception. Everything – from eating breakfast, to going to the loo and having sex with their partner – is streamed live online to an audience of millions. What sort of person would accept such terms in order to enjoy supreme power? How might they subvert it?

9 2024: Google becomes a self-aware Artificial Intelligence. Predicated as it is upon 'the search', it dedicates itself to finding the answer to the universe's most profound questions. On 1 January 2025 it announces that it has proven conclusively and once and for all whether or not God exists. At once, military strikes are launched upon its main banks of computation to prevent it disseminating this knowledge ...

10 In the twenty-second century, several new genders become popular, including bigender, neut-gender, tri-gender, supergender and cyclogender. By the early twenty-third century,

old-fashioned 'female' and 'male' humans have become an oppressed minority …

11 A lone researcher uncovers the mystery of music – a super-rational mathematical species of alien had devised it three thousand years earlier, as a means of infiltrating the (to them) baffling and alarming 'emotional' minds of human beings. After long-gestated development, music is almost at the stage when these beings will be able to use it wholly to control and therefore conquer *Homo sapiens* …

12 An alien makes certain very large demands of the Earth; unless these demands are met, the alien promises he will reconfigure pi across a select area of the globe, making it exactly 3. At first his threat is laughingly dismissed, but then he makes it happen in a thousand-kilometre-wide oval of land in north America. All engines built around circular components fail; wheels break apart; rain dissolves in a freezing mist. A second strike in China has similar results. The alien ups its demands, threatening to apply its power across the whole circularly defined globe, causing it to disintegrate. Can this threat be countered? Can the alien be stopped in time?

13 In the future, prominent football matches are played with key players made available for 'seat jockeys' to operate. The players are human, but with certain prosthetic augmentations enabling a third party to control arms and legs via a game pad. People pay high fees to 'play' in (for instance) World Cup matches at this remove, like gamers of old – and the players receive very substantial fees for allowing themselves to be 'puppetized' in this way. But when the world's top scorer is arrested for murder, he insists that he was not in control of his actions at the time …

14 One hot summer's day the Thames unexpectedly, and abruptly, freezes solid from Tower Bridge up to Chelsea Bridge. How has it happened? What technology is at play? Where has the power come from, and who is in control of it?

15 God reveals himself, in ways that cannot be disavowed or ignored, in all his glory. But, he announces, Christianity, Islam, Hinduism, Judaism – all of them have misunderstood his essence. Instead he declares: Richard Dawkins is the New Messiah. Then he departs. What happens next …?

16 Two rival space elevators are being constructed in the tropics; one – built from conventional materials, on the island of Madagascar, is a steel, neo-plastic and monofilament engineering project on an epic scale, funded by a consortium of the world's twenty-second-century superpowers (China, Brazil, USA and EU). The other, on a Pacific island, is the project of an eccentric trillionaire. She claims to have developed new technology that will grow the elevator shaft *naturally*, a process halfway between a beanstalk and a special kind of crystal. At first the world powers dismiss this as a ludicrous vanity project; soon, though, the Pacific elevator outpaces the African one. Attempts to surveil the construction are sabotaged. And then the structure appears to become sentient, aware ... and hostile!

17 One day the world wakes to a sky that is bright green.

18 An alien force prepares to invade the Earth by throwing a force field around the planet that prevents effective REM sleep – and waits. After a week, the first people start going insane; after a fortnight people are dropping dead. Can Earthly scientists, in an increasingly exhausted race against time, find a cure – or organize a fight back – in time?

19 A dystopian world, or prison colony, where fingers are money – cut one off and exchange it for enough credits for a year's provisions. You can exchange another person's finger, but only with their express permission – the currency exchange needs to see them 'gift' the finger to you in person.

20 Neurophages from a nerve-agent attack during some future war have entered the water table. People are afflicted with crippling levels of embarrassment, to the point where they cannot function physically, fall to the ground weeping and so on – the effect attaching itself to a variety of circumstances (which might be, for example, eating and watching others eat, smiling, music, daylight ...).

21 A scientist working on teleportation has reached the point where he can teleport viruses; but he despairs of ever being able to bring the monumental processing power to bear on the task of teleporting a mouse or cat – let alone a whole human being. His funding has run out. The military, however, is very interested in the idea of teleporting viruses into the bodies of enemy soldiers, and offers to fund his further studies. He faces

an ethical dilemma: should he allow the military to take over his research?

22 It is discovered that telepathy only happens when exactly the right four susceptible people come together. The gene responsible is widely scattered around the globe, and until very recently in human history the chances of exactly the right four people from (say) China, North America, Europe and Africa getting together was vanishingly small. Nonetheless, it sometimes happened, and the telepathic 'pod' would swiftly achieve great things. With international travel these 'pods' more often come together, so much so that by the mid-twenty-first century they are becoming a clear and present threat to the global status quo …

23 A zookeeper introduces a group of schoolchildren to the zoo's celebrated eagle. The eagle carries one of the children away to a magical kingdom.

24 A princess gives your protagonist a magic pomegranate. S/he eats the fruit and spits out the seeds, but when each seed touches the ground it sprouts into a man. When a dozen men have assembled around your protagonist they suddenly seize him/her and carry him/her away.

25 An alien intelligence makes humankind an offer: it will gift us the technology to travel to the stars, but only if we agree – all of us, without exception – to give up our sexual desire (something the intelligence finds repellent). The removal of all sexual desire will be a simple matter for the aliens and painless for us; and the government assures us that it will still be possible to harvest sperm and implant fertilized eggs, so our species will not die out. Without this, we will be condemned to live our existence trapped in a backwater. Should we accept?

26 For as-yet-unexplained reasons, all the world's ice vanishes overnight. As 90 per cent of icebergs lie below the water's surface, this actually results in a slight reduction of the global water coverage, resulting in ultra-low tides and uncovering large tracts of land – especially in the Antarctic.

27 In a *Matrix*-style virtual reality, six separate realms have all been programmed to resemble twentieth-century Soviet Russia. One of these kingdoms is programmed to be destroyed in an apocalyptic cometary impact if our protagonist enters it; the

other five are safe. But in one of them (our protagonist does not know which) lies the MacGuffin code, vital to the continuing survival of actual humanity outside the simulation ...

28 A far future galactic empire is faced with the ultimate doomsday weapon – a small 'reality code' that, dropped into a black hole, momentarily reverses the arrow of gravitational force, causing everything locked within the singularity to explode violently outwards. Entire star systems are destroyed in the battle against this weapon; but can the Galactic Marine Corps prevent it being fired into the supermassive black hole at the centre of the galaxy, thereby destroying the entire empire ...?

29 A time traveller sets off for the Holy Land at the time of Christ with a high-powered rifle. His plan? To shoot Jesus – but only after he has resurrected himself from death after the crucifixion, and before he ascends to heaven. 'He has conquered death and is therefore unkillable – and I shall prove it!' A team of time commandos is sent to stop him ...

30 In a future society, sleep has been abolished. To avoid the deleterious effects of sleep deprivation, the physiological and mental needs of sleep are attended to by certain carefully designed processor implants in the brain tissue. Now worker productivity can be doubled, and nobody need sleep. Worker XC224 is a contented, productive member of this world until one day his friend offers him a new and very illegal drug, one that shuts off the implants and allows the user to sleep ...

31 You are in a blissful relationship with the love of your life. But one day you discover that you have a telepathic connection with a third party. You didn't ask for it, and didn't seek it out, but once you are aware of it you cannot ignore it. This telepathic link gives you an intimacy with the third party you can never achieve with your actual life partner, and there's something in that which is almost overwhelmingly compelling. How will this triangle shake down, narrative-wise?

32 King Midas, seated in his palace, has his wish answered – everything he touches turns to gold. The couch he is sitting on turns to gold; the clothes he is wearing turn to gold; the air inside his lungs turns to gold (killing him, of course). Fortunately for the world, the windows of the palace are sealed, and this auric transformation limits itself to the air inside. But

what happens when the wish is asked for, and granted, outside? The end of the world! The chase is on to find the source of this catastrophically dangerous magic and stop it!

33 A super-wealthy space merchant builds an exact, life-size replica of the Copernican solar system around a nuclear-fusion sun, and then invites several million of the galaxy's poorest and most desperate citizens to live luxurious lives inside it. The catch is that they must worship him as a god.

3 DEVELOPMENT DIRECTIONS

1 Aggregate the story by bringing in more and more characters.

2 De-aggregate the story by killing off or otherwise removing more characters.

3 Set a tight deadline, with suitably dire consequences if your protagonist does not meet it. Then find a reason in the story to halve the deadline. Then halve it again.

4 Decide in advance how many 'plot coupons' (to use Nick Lowe's brilliant coinage) your character must collect before s/he is able to 'cash in' the story's conclusion. Identify what the coupons are, and have your character collect them.

5 Dispense with the very notion of 'plot coupons', and write a fluid, experimental stream-of-consciousness-style narration.

6 Send the protagonist on a lengthy quest (see Chapter 8).

7 Have the protagonist's love-object kidnapped by a sandman, a dragon, a Balrog, or conceivably by all three acting in cahoots.

8 Engineer a crisis that threatens the very stability of reality!

9 Follow the characters through the perfectly humdrum routines of a succession of regular days, introducing a new anomaly each day until the number of anomalies begins to overwhelm normalcy.

10 Throw the antagonist at the protagonist as many times as you need to get the story up and running smoothly.

4 STROPHE

Your strophe, or turn, or reveal, should proceed organically from your premise. It might be that a key character is revealed to be quite different from what s/he appeared (if good, then revealed as the villain;

if the villain, then vice versa; if powerless, powerful; if mad, sane; if unimportant, important; and so on) or that a key event, artefact or prop has been previously misinterpreted or overlooked; or...

5 DENOUEMENT

1 Everyone dies.

2 Everyone thinks they are going to die, but at the last minute disaster is averted and they live.

3 A god comes out of the machine.

4 The protagonist awakes to find that everything was a dream – a dream in which Philip K. Dick uses the *Enterprise's* Holodeck to act out scenes from *The Matrix*.

5 It was the robo-butler!

6 The ring is thrown into the volcano, but instead of being destroyed it dissolves and infects the lava with evil. Magma bursts out to create a circular formation of magically malign granite hillocks.

7 The Dark Lord is defeated, but with his dying breath reveals that your protagonist, Lord Nazilot, was evil all along – and that Dara K. Lord was fighting him on behalf of the forces of goodness!

8 Song and dance number or custard pie fight.

9 The denouement reveals one key element in the story to have been otherwise than the reader has hitherto assumed it to be. Revealing this upends all.

10 The ending turns out to be the beginning! It's all an ouroboros worm biting its own tail. And why wouldn't the worm bite its tail? Its tail tastes of chocolate.

11 The ending is gloriously oblique and avant garde.

12 The ending brings poetic justice. Poetry itself is hauled into the dock and found guilty of fraudulently misrepresenting the prosaic nature of reality. An exemplary sentence is on the cards.

13 End on a pun.

14 Exeunt, pursued by a bear. An alien bear. Or perhaps a were-bear. Assuming your characters are aware there's a were-bear there.

15 The story simply stops.

Index